The Guide to Everlasting Employability

Sarah

love ya!

miss ya!

See you soon!

Linda xxx

Sarah

Y'r a very special person

thanks for all your support

Michael

The Authors

Michael Moran is Chief Executive of 10Eighty. He is an expert in helping people manage their careers, having worked in the National Health Service, Insurance, Commodities and Derivatives industries. In the last 15 years Michael has run businesses that have helped 75,000 people make successful career transitions.

He is a frequent commentator in the press/media. Most recent media mentions have included BBC South, CNBC, Radio4, Financial Times, City AM, Financial News, Evening Standard, The Sunday Times, Executive Grapevine and HR Magazine. He writes a careers column for People Management, a blog for the Human Resources Magazine and is a regular contributor to The Thompson Reuters HR Portal.

Michael spent 2011 writing this book, launching an iPhone app "careers snakes and ladders" and designing an online interactive version of the book in collaboration with Marshall ACM to coincide with the launch of his new business.

Michael has a degree in Economics, an MBA from Warwick Business School and is a Fellow of the Chartered Institute of Personnel and Development.

Michael's linked profile: Http://uk.linked in.com/in/michaeldmoran
You can follow Michael on twitter: mdmoran10Eighty
Michael's career blog can be found at www.michaeldmoran.blogspot.com

Linda Jackson is Managing Director and Co-Founder of 10Eighty.

Linda was previously a main board director of Savile plc, the career and talent management AIM listed plc for 8 years and latterly Managing Director of Fairplace Cedar Ltd. She has studied and worked in career management for the last 20 years and is recognised as a strong practitioner as a Career Management professional and coach. Working with people on one to one basis continues to be a personal passion alongside running a business with her fellow directors.

With a relevant BSc degree in Management Sciences from Manchester University, majoring in finance, law and psychology, she built her career through various positions in the public sector before turning to the city and banking. Her former career was in military intelligence.

She is a frequent commentator in the press, including CNBC both in London and the Middle East, Radio 5 Live, Financial Times, City AM, Financial News, Evening Standard, The Sunday Times and The Executive Grapevine.

Linda's LinkedIn profile can be found at: http://uk.linkedin.com/pub/linda-jackson/1/461/765
Follow her on Twitter: LindaJ_10Eighty

The Guide to Everlasting Employability

Michael Moran
Linda Jackson

First published by
10Eighty Limited
107–111 Fleet Street
London
EC4A 2AB

http://www.10eighty.co.uk

The authors gratefully acknowledge Ted Goff for the cartoons. All reasonable efforts have been made to contact other copyright holders.

Cover design by aidan traynor
www.primedesign.co.uk/aidantraynor

Editorial and publishing services by Lumax Consultancy Limited

In memory of Beryl and Rosemary

"You've got to find what you love and that is as true for work as it is for lovers. Your work is going to fill a large part of your life and the only way to be truly satisfied is to do what you believe is great work. And the only way to do great work is to love what you do. If you haven't found it yet, keep looking and don't settle. As with all matters of the heart, you'll know when you've found it."

Steve Jobs

Thank You's

As always there are lots of people to thank and without whom this book would not have been possible.

Helen Menhenett for helping me take the first steps in writing this book. Linda Jackson and Nick Lawson for helping me take the final steps and without whom the book would not have been finished.

Dave Harrison and Liz Sebag-Montefiore, my co-founders of 10Eighty. It is truly a pleasure to spend time with you.

Joan, my wife: The best decision I ever made.

Enjoy: please take the lessons to heart.

I am constantly surprised how little people know about this employability business and yet they spend so much time in work.

I am truly blessed. I do what I love.

I wish you the same.

Michael Moran

Working with people who inspire you is something many people would envy. I am delighted that Michael asked me to become involved with this project and helping him write this book has been a great source of pleasure and debate. Working around the 10Eighty board table with Michael and fellow directors Liz, Dave and Nick with their combined wit and intelligence also makes the job not only worthwhile but a constant joy.

Other great sources of inspiration during the course of this project have come from my immediate family, my children, my clients and my friends, some old and some new - you know who you are!

And finally! A quote by the American Poet Mary Oliver:

"Tell me, what it is that you plan to do with your one wild and precious life?"

A question that I think is worth us all reviewing !

Linda Jackson

Table of Contents

Appendices

Introduction

The aim of this book

"I skate to where the puck is going to be, not to where it has been."
Wayne Gretzky

This book is designed as a guide to help you to plan your career so as to guarantee success now and in the future.

If you bought the book then, thank you. Work with it the way that suits you. It's a short book but it should be useful over and over as you review and manage your career. Perhaps not all the sections are relevant to you at the moment. Choose the bits you are interested in and want to focus on. After all, building a career is the project of a lifetime.

Career planning is a skill you can learn. This book aims to give you practical advice and tools to learn about proactive career management. It's not meant to be a quick fix; a one-off read that you then leave on the shelf. It should be useful throughout your career. Every time you do a Career MOT you'll need the book.

One assumption that we are making is that you have to work because you need the money. Building a career is about sustenance. You have to live. But we know self-made millionaires who still need a challenging "occupation". So either way, you need to think about your employability and who is going to pay for your skills, knowledge, and expertise. Do you have the skills that are in demand? How employable are you? Not just now but in the future?

The book was written because it seems to us that working life shouldn't just be about the money. Money is important but not as important as job satisfaction. We spend so much time working and so few people really enjoy it. That's a real shame. So this book has been written by me and my business partner, Linda Jackson. We have worked with thousands of people over the years and this book is the output of many years of experience that we've gained and would like to share with you. As a result you may notice that we use the term "we" or "I" as virtually interchangeable!

How many people do you know who look forward to work? I firmly believe everybody can and should have a happy, successful career doing something they love, doing it well, contributing to society and having fun while they do it.

If you are serious about career planning and making changes then you'll make the time to read the book and do the exercises. We didn't want to scatter planning grids and exercises throughout the book but there are places where you might want to stop, dog-ear the page, check the appendices, think about what you've read. Take time to reflect on what you've read and to discuss it with a mentor or career coach.

Why this self-help book will work

Most people make most things too complicated, most of the time. I hope this book is clear and to the point. It aims to kick-start your success. It aims to give you a starting point and it includes space to make notes and write down self-help action plans. It is about career motivation and identifying your drive to succeed.

The motivation to make a change will enable you to help yourself. Just reading the book won't make a jot of difference. It's a book, not a magic wand.

In his book *How to Stop Worrying and Start Living*, Dale Carnegie recommends his readers do the following:

1. Cultivate a deep driving desire to learn because you will gain profound satisfaction and confidence from it.
2. Speed read each chapter and then revisit, reread thoroughly, then do the exercises.
3. Stop frequently in your reading and reflect. Ask yourself just how and when you can apply each suggestion.
4. It's okay to underline anything you feel is important. Indeed I encourage you to do so.
5. Return to the book. Keep it somewhere prominent so you see it every day. Reread; dip in and out frequently.
6. We learn by doing - learning is an active process.
7. See your mistakes as part of the learning process. No one's career journey is right first time, so expect career cul de sacs. Learn from your mistakes.
8. To help the reflective process, write it down. Keep a diary. Pontificate on what you have learnt and intend to do about it.

In the words of the Spice Girls: "What do you really, really want?" Using this book is a bit like a partnership and it requires you to be motivated and take action.

If you have ever come across Kolb's Learning Cycle you'll know this to be true: You try something, you reflect on how it went, you consider improvements and you try it again. You won't ever improve your golf swing by reading a book. You have to swing the club and hit the ball. Practise makes perfect - and it's the same with this book. Reading it won't make a jot of difference unless you put what you learn into action. We'll remind you every now and again!

The purpose of the book is to help you plan your career. What I would regard as a successful career will comprise three things:

1. Career success enjoyment.
2. Lifelong employability.
3. Job satisfaction.

While you enjoy your successful career, remember the three over-arching aims of the career plan are that you should

- have fun,
- make money, and
- do some good.

But you have to help yourself. You have to learn and then act on that learning if you want to grow and improve and better yourself. Nobody else can do it for you. Relying on HR to look after your career for you would be a mistake. Even with the best of intentions, they don't know you like you do. Besides, your aspirations may change over time and they won't necessarily know that.

Reading advice and theories, setting a programme for change, resolving to do better, are all very well but what you want is actual improvement. That's why most self-help books don't work for most people. Because actually putting the advice into practice is optional. Long-term behavioural change takes work. It's not easy to change the habits of a lifetime.

To start with, you need to understand yourself, your drives and motivators. You have to examine your likes and dislikes, honestly and rigorously. Likewise your values, skills and interests and own up to what you really, really want. Then you have to make an effort to get whatever it is you say you really want, otherwise success will never be a reality for you.

If you aren't prepared to make the effort to get what you want then probably you won't get it. Does it matter? Not to anyone else. If you don't have sufficient self-belief and drive to get what you want then how much did you really want it?

If you don't really want it after all, that's fine too. There is no point striving for something you don't want. Why waste the energy? So you have to acknowledge the difference between wanting to do something and actually doing it in real time.

Getting what you want is its own reward. Talk is cheap but I believe that you can do anything if you set your mind to it. Set a goal and aim for it.

And another thing: Decide at the outset what success looks like.

Set your goals, write them down. Articulate your objectives: Discuss them with your mentor, with your friends, your partner. Focus on what you want to achieve. Review your goals regularly. Remind yourself of them, and revise them when necessary. Be positive about your achievements, your outstanding objectives, and your failures to date. Whilst you can learn from mistakes, don't be crushed by them. Life isn't perfect so focus on the positive and think about how to achieve more.

You need to work with what you learn and apply that learning to your life as you go along. That's how you develop and grow. Reflecting on what you've learned, as you act on advice, changes you and gives you the tools to make more change happen.

Visualising success, where you want to be, how you want to build and shape your career and future is great. In addition, though, you need an action plan and the relevant skills to back that. And you need to commit to that success – time, money, emotional investment, effort, tenacity, courage, networking – it may take more than you first thought! Nothing ventured, nothing gained.

It's a simple technique, but visualising success really works. I'm told that David Beckham, when playing in what is considered his finest match for England against Greece in 2002, used this technique. They were three minutes into injury time and he had a free kick, thirty yards from goal. He scored. This goal meant that England qualified in the World Cup Finals.

Two aspects of the situation illustrate the essence of what I believe is important for success: the first, is that he believed he was due to score. He had failed with several previous free kicks and knew it was time he nailed one because he practices assiduously. Secondly, he visualised the goal; he remembered how he'd been lambasted by the press for his failure at St. Etienne in the previous World Cup and imagined how it would be if his goal set us up for success and a place in the next World Cup with Beckham as the team's saviour. So, in effect

- practice to get better – luck is not enough, perfect your skills;
- visualise success – set the stage and imagine yourself succeeding; and
- focus and act.

If you want to change or improve some aspect of your life or career, don't try to do it all by yourself. Sure, you got the book, but more importantly, get a helper. You can't delegate motivation, but having someone to bounce ideas off and to help you keep on track is invaluable. Get a mentor such as a senior colleague or career coach to support you and encourage you.

Role models can be a powerful force for learning and realising your potential. They're not only important for your career, but for achieving fulfilment in everything you do. You ought to have role models at every stage of your life.

The only thing holding you back is you. The important thing is taking the first step as Lao-tzu, the Chinese philosopher, observed: "The journey of a thousand miles begins with a single step."

Chapter 1

The New Employment Paradigm

"You don't have to be great to start, but you have to start to be great."

Zig Ziglar

What this chapter tells you about Everlasting Employability:

- The new career paradigm: mobility and learning agility.
- How to plan a possible career path.
- The importance of shared values and culture.

Let's start with a question. What is the difference between working for one company for 15 years or for three different companies in the same sector over 15 years? It is a factor of working for the competition. If you do the latter then the chances are that you will be paid more, you'll have more confidence about your transferable skills and as a result your employability will be enhanced.

These days if you are just starting out, it may be foolish to align your career to one company. That's old style thinking. Three different jobs mean you will be more employable long term because you have a better understanding of the industry as a whole and it's that market intelligence that makes you valuable.

So the new career strategy for the aspiring executive is firstly to get a good education - stay in school. Go to university if you can; yes it will cost you £50,000 but the return on investment will be many times that over your lifetime. If you can, take a gap year; go travelling, experience different cultures. You will have a much better understanding of global issues and will develop more confidence as a result. If you are already established in your career and do not feel say, an MBA, is appropriate, then the message is simple - remain open minded to learning and considering new ways of doing things. Invest in yourself or risk becoming a dinosaur!

Education is important because it teaches you to question, evaluate and reason. It's about spending time around others who don't think in the same way that you do. Most learning is experiential. In *The Leadership Machine* by Lombardo and Eichinger, they note that development is about discomfort because "comfort is the enemy of growth. Staying in our comfort zone encourages repetition. Going against the grain, being forced or venturing outside of the cosy boxes of our lives demands that we learn". So a dynamic competitive environment is often challenging and frequently uncomfortable.

There are three prerequisites for career success in the modern workplace:

1. A reasonably high IQ or intelligence is important but not enough on its own to guarantee success; we know that the brightest people are not always the most successful.
2. EQ or emotional intelligence is about how well you relate to other people, the social skills that you will need for team roles and leadership roles. It's important and will increase your chances of success, but you also need.
3. Learning agility - more so than ever before, you need to be able to work and manage in fast-changing environments. The sort of environments where you can't just apply the old ways of working and thinking because 9 times out of 10 they are no longer applicable or relevant. This is where the ability to analyse and evaluate and change direction when needed is invaluable.

During your 20's, your aim is to work for two or three, maybe four, companies for between18 months to 2 1/2 years each. Where possible, try and find roles in recognised brand leaders; organisations that will help you grow and develop your potential. You need to look for roles that will stretch and challenge you and help you decide what you enjoy and what you want from the world of work.

"I'm seeking a job with low
stress, interesting coworkers,
a pleasant office and a fun boss.
What do you have?"

This first series of jobs are all-important in your 20s because they brand your CV. For example, what is the difference between Virgin Rail and Network Rail? Virgin Rail is seen as sexy, modern and attached to Sir Richard Branson, a marketing guru; Network Rail is seen as an organisation full of engineers that doesn't have the same cache. Irony on irony, they are in the same line of business, one sets-up the tracks and the other puts the trains on them.

The other aspect about big employment brands is that they have powerful alumni groups. And groups like the PWC, Deloitte and McKinsey alumni will be invaluable in your later career. This is also why, if you are aiming high, it's good at some stage in your career to get an MBA from a top ten business school. People value the brand name of a good business school and it gives you great alumni contacts. However, networking is a key concept that we will return to in the book and the good news is that it works at every level. If you feel you are not cut out for academia, you can still demonstrate a desire to continue to learn.

The key point at this stage is that if you have decided on a specific sector, then target the major players in that field. If you are a functional specialist, an accountant, marketing manager, or HR professional then working for a recognised company is important.

Working overseas is important too – because, again, it develops your learning agility. We learn fastest when we are working in an unfamiliar environment. Your skill in responding to different trends and environments increases with practice, so if you have worked in three or four different environments you will have more learning agility.

If you are not an experienced senior hand, an MBA is important because it teaches you the fundamentals of business. You need to understand what drives a business both in micro terms - competitors and local markets - and macro terms - what is happening in the world in which the business operates.

A good example of changing market conditions is as follows: if you worked for Walkers Crisps ten years ago you probably didn't worry about obesity. Today you have to respond to different customer concerns; society has changed, the questions your customers ask have changed and their demands on your product range have changed.

Have you walked past a branch of McDonalds recently? They've gone green, literally. This is not a coincidence. They have had to respond to the concerns their customers expressed about the environment, nutritional health and animal welfare.

If you go to business school you will spend time with people like you - bright people, but because they are from different sectors and geographies and cultures, working with them will help you become a well-rounded person.

You develop learning agility when you are working with and learning from others. On an MBA course you all work on the same problem but bring different perspectives to bear on the question and identify different possible solutions. The value lies in learning to consider and evaluate different points of view. It teaches you divergent thinking as opposed to convergent thinking - in other words to search for realistic options rather than the most obvious solution.

In the early stages of your career you're finding your way round, testing the waters and working out what sort of culture suits you best. At this stage in your career you can be adventurous, take overseas secondments, take a sabbatical to travel or work on aid projects, or consider an MBA. You are weighing up your values and exploring new avenues and working out your route to a fulfilling career and a lifestyle that suits you.

After job-hopping and working for a number of competing companies, by the time you get to your late 20s and early 30s you need to decide what is right for you for the next ten years.

Surprise, surprise, this is also the time when, typically, family and children start to make a really big difference to what you want from life. Your ability to be mobile changes and you may want to spend more time in one place with one company.

A key decision is picking an organisation or industry which aligns with your values. You could be the best marketing director in the world and a passionate anti-smoker, but if you are, you won't feel entirely comfortable at British American Tobacco.

The most significant career de-railer is where you find yourself working for people or an organisation where you don't have the same value system. There is no hiding place in this situation, it will find you out! So if you are thinking long-term you need to get that right.

In your 30s you should be making the most of your achievements, having developed a strong bank of core competencies and, most importantly, built your network. You should have aligned yourself to people one or two levels above you who are fast trackers. Work on impressing them because when they move within the industry they will take you with them.

This is also the time when you could be putting down the building blocks of wealth creation - share options and equity participation.

Never ignore a chance to learn and grow. Goal-setting, exploring career options, researching market trends so you are well prepared - all these skills will benefit your life as well as your career path! Stephen Covey in "The Seven Habits of Highly Successful People" studied executives and found that the most successful wrote down their goals and reviewed them periodically. So, write down those goals!

If you're lucky you will choose the right route and find a career you love and start climbing the ladder of success. But if you are not there yet, don't worry, it's not too late to change. In your 30s you start to develop the career you nurtured during your 20s.

As we get older, our needs change and we may need to revise the career plan accordingly. We may find a partner, buy a home and have children. Children, especially, change everything, forever. By now you should be more focussed, having sown seeds and put down roots.

By the end of your 30s you should know where you are heading over the next 10 to 15 years. You have transferable skills and valuable expertise. Competitor companies may be interested in you.

This is an interesting time. With luck, you will have enjoyed your early career but the rules of the game now change. And because hopefully, in the scheme of things, you have had some success and have a measure of financial independence, you can see light at the end of tunnel. Now you can start taking a different view about what you do. You can develop options.

The value is very much in you, the individual, not the organisation. Financial independence will allow you to take your skill set and apply it in a different way if you choose. Do you want to take the risk? Can you see yourself in a role outside the organisation? It could be time, if you feel you have exhausted your career, to reinvent yourself.

Don't hesitate to do an in-depth review if you feel you have reached this point. Get a mentor and get some feedback. Tap into a rich vein of expertise and experience.

Taking into account your interests, values and skills, you may have the option to move from one occupation into another. Probably you will have to re-train. So do some research before you make that move.

What you must not do is subside into thinking, without questioning it, "I am going to spend the next 20 years in the same profession".

See your career as having a shelf life. Once you are in your 50s you might decide to do something different – perhaps a portfolio career or working for yourself.

If you always wanted to run your own business, this is the time to go for it. You might be contemplating a second career. When values change then you may decide to take a different direction. Bankers become teachers. Secretaries become landscape gardeners. Take a close look at your wants, needs, aspirations and make sure your skills and plans are aligned with your values. It takes nerve to make a successful career change but do your research and persevere. The rewards of reinventing yourself will make the move worth it.

In summary, the new employment paradigm requires you in the first phase of your career to work in recognised brands. Brands that will look good on your CV. The second phase requires you to lay down a track record - so you know what you want to do, you know what you are good at and you build your reputation in that space. The third phase, now you are in your fifties, will be the time to start thinking about a portfolio career or maybe running your own business. Career success comes from having a career plan and sharing your plans with your network.

Part 1

The medium to long term:
What you need to be doing

Chapter 2

The Career MOT

"There are no secrets to success. It is the result of preparation, hard work, and learning from failure."

Colin Powell, former US Secretary of State

What this chapter tells you about Everlasting Employability:

- Blind loyalty leads to career obsolescence.

- How to carry out a Career MOT.

- Focus on your strengths; get feedback.

- What to do if you are in the wrong place.

- The power of objective setting.

- The power of career conversations and how to close gaps.

- Being proactive.

- It's not about how old you are.

- 3 prerequisites for career success.

The car analogy regarding the MOT is a good one because you need to take time out and carry out a self-appraisal on a regular basis. Is your career on track? Is the direction you are going in still the right one? As an asset are you appreciating? Do you really have 25 years of experience? Or is it, in reality, about one year's worth of experience replicated 25 times?

It is your responsibility to manage your career. It is not the responsibility of the organisation you work for to do that, though they may have career and talent management policies and programmes. They may be good at engaging and developing staff; if they are not, you should be looking around anyway, but your career is down to you.

Don't be beguiled into thinking that being loyal will be sufficient. Organisations can be ruthless with regards to disposing of assets they no longer need. In the end, they can't afford to be philanthropic.

A Career MOT is a good idea if any of the following apply:

- Your job lacks challenge.

- Promotion or development opportunities are limited.

- You're not learning anything new; it's all routine.

- You feel your talent and skill are being wasted.

- You are stressed or depressed.

- You feel unappreciated, unengaged, disconnected.

- Work is no longer fun.

"My shortcomings? I'm
sometimes too inquisitive.
What are your shortcomings?"

Perhaps you feel you've reached a career ceiling but still have the drive and tenacity to rise further. You want to move on to fresh challenges and higher levels of creativity. Keeping your career afloat may feel like you're navigating hazardous and murky waters, especially during times of company mergers and acquisitions, downsizing, 'right sizing,' and 'off-shoring'.

The Career MOT will take time but you don't have to hurry. You need thinking time as well as an action plan. Go with the ebb and flow, take time to focus and reflect every now and then. Nothing is set in stone. The career plan you envisaged when you were 23 may no longer be relevant now. That's fine. You can start over.

We all like to do things in different ways. If you like observation, planning, reflecting, considering things, then that's probably reflected in the work you choose to do and the jobs you do well. If you like experimenting, fixing things, decision-making then you work in a different way, so be aware of your preferences and strengths. Play to those strengths.

This strengths based approach is fundamental. If you take what you do well and do more of it then you are more likely to succeed. Self-knowledge is crucial. Otherwise how can you decide what you will want to be doing in 5 years' time?

In the rest of this chapter are several exercises designed to help you "know yourself". Start with the SWOT analysis and the Reflected Best Self™ exercise detailed below, as it can help you decide where you should be going.

Simple exercises such as examining your skills and values or plotting out a career line will help you work out how you spend your time, what is important to you, what you are good at and what you have enjoyed in your career to date.

The exercises should give you some ideas and help you identify some answers. Take time for some rigorous self-analysis on your career and skills to date.

SWOT analysis

Use the SWOT framework below to separate yourself from your peers, and analyse the specialist talents and abilities you need to advance your career.

Strengths	Weaknesses
What you are good at	What you are not good at
Opportunities	**Threats**
Skills in demand	Changes that might make you redundant

Be as objective as you can. This is no time for false modesty. You are unique. We all have talent but we don't all recognise or use our talent to its full potential much of the time. There's a table in the Appendix at the back that you can use to map this out.

Reflected Best Self™

This is another exercise to help identify your unique strengths and talents. It's a great tool for personal development and was designed at the University of Michigan Business School.

The idea is to ask for positive feedback from significant people in your life and then use it to build a cumulative portrait of your "best self."

Reflected Best Self is better in many instances than a full 360 degree feedback exercise because positive feedback is really helpful and people's strengths tend to be hard-wired. A focus on weaknesses doesn't really lead us to work on those weaknesses; in fact, negative feedback generally puts us on the defensive.

Conversely, most people respond well to praise, even when they think, or know, it is unwarranted. It's nice to be appreciated and we'll repeat behaviour that generated positive feedback in the hope of getting more. This is our version of the Reflected Best Self tool.

How to use the tool

Identify ten or so people to give you constructive feedback about your strengths. Try to include current colleagues and also, ideally, former colleagues, friends and family members. Tell them what you are aiming to find out so that they know you are not just fishing for compliments. You could try doing this as a group exercise if it's convenient.

Ask them to think about your strengths and to give an example of each strength they identify. This doesn't have to be specifically work-related. In fact, if you're planning a change of role it may be useful that you get feedback from people who know you outside the work context, as they may pinpoint strengths that you have which you're not able to display at work.

Once you have collated the results you can look for themes and profile them so you can play to your strengths. You'll find that Reflected Best Self provides a great deal of food for thought. You'll get back unexpected comments that will boost your confidence and make you think about how you work and the impression you make on your colleagues and peers. New and unexpected information like this can be a real catalyst for changing the way we view things and do things, enabling us to look at ourselves in a new light.

The Reflected Best Self exercise is based on a strengths-based personal development model. This model is comprehensively explained in *Now, Discover your Strengths* by Marcus Buckingham and Donald O. Clifton, (2001).

The career line exercise
This exercise uses a lifeline graphic representation of your personal history, with all its ups and downs.

1. Draw your own career line by drawing a line across the middle of a large sheet of paper, marking the years along the bottom since leaving college or school and continuing to the present day.

2. Score each role out of from +10 to -10 in terms of job satisfaction, achievements and plot them on the page. Join the dots!

3. Review your career lifeline. Look at its shape. Are there many highs or lows? Is your line jagged or flat? Why? What was it specifically that made this phase a high or a low? Are there any recurring themes that created high or low job satisfaction? Does the line suggest any patterns?

4. Record what you have learned about yourself.

You could also add your personal lifeline by plotting life events. Using a different coloured pen do the same exercise on the same sheet and compare the two lines. Sometimes factors extraneous to your career impact on your professional life, e.g. family illnesses may upset work life balance or the arrival of children may change on the amount of time you want to spend in the office.

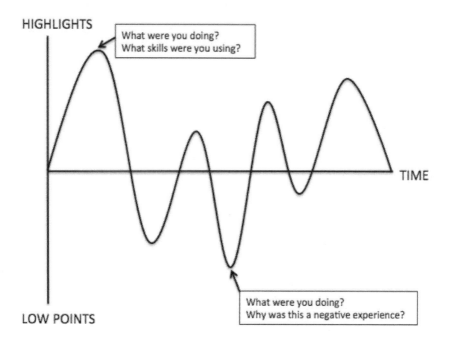

Ask yourself the following questions:

1. What is the relationship between your career and your life as a whole?
2. How close are the lines during the highest and lowest periods?
3. Do you see any tensions or conflicts?
4. What do your career and personal lifelines say about the role of work in your life?

Broken career?

What if you are totally in the wrong space? Is there anything you can do? Go back to fundamentals. What do you like doing? Think about your achievements to date and think big, don't be modest. Life is full of achievements, big and small.

We tend to take things for granted as we get older. Well you have our permission to give yourself some credit for what you do well. List your achievements and reflect back on the past and what you did well, what you enjoyed learning and doing.

Give yourself some space to consider how you got into a situation or a role that is not right for you. What can you do about it? What are you willing to do to get what you want? What will you give up to achieve what you really like from life?

If you are going to make a complete career change, be sure to stick a toe in the water before you make a big leap. Get some work experience, do a try-out, shadow somebody. Over time we have met several City derivatives traders who thought it might be a good idea to get off the treadmill and "put something back". They did teacher training courses and went off to teach maths. Some will tell you it's the best career move they ever made but others found that they simply hated teaching.

So if, for example, you think you want to be a teacher, arrange to spend a Friday afternoon helping the teaching assistants at your local school. It could be an eye-opener.

Once we have been in the workplace for a while we tend to develop a pretty good idea of what we don't want to do. Fixing on a new direction is harder but playing to your strengths is a good bet. So do the Reflected Best Self exercise presented above and try to get a fresh perspective on your career.

Learning to make the best of you

Your learning preference may also have an impact on career choice.

Learning happens when we experience an event which causes us to stop and think. We mentioned Kolb in our introductory section. He identified four stages in the learning process and although it is depicted as circular (as shown below), all of us have a preference as to where we like to spend our time. For example, you will hear some people talk about preferring to be hands on and actively engaged in a task as the best way to learn. Others will prefer to think through all the aspects and possibilities and to analyse and reflect.

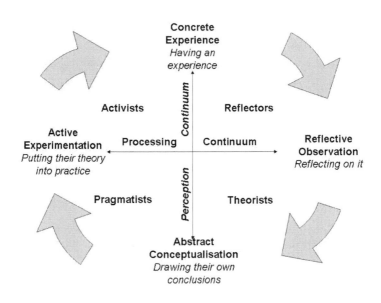

These preferences have impact on our career choice, for example traders or broadcasters who like to work in the moment are likely to be Activists. Peter Honey and Alan Mumford built on Kolb's model and identified four main learning style types:

- Activist
- Reflector
- Theorist
- Pragmatist

These types are described as follows:

- An Activist prefers the challenges of new experiences, involvement with others, assimilation and role-playing. Likes anything new, problem solving and small group discussions.

- A Reflector prefers to watch, think and review what has happened. Likes to use journals and brainstorming. Lectures are helpful if they provide expert explanations and analysis.

- A Theorist prefers to think problems through in a step-by-step manner. Likes lectures, analogies, systems, case studies, models and reading. Talking with experts is normally less helpful.

- A Pragmatist prefers to apply new learning in practice to see if it works. Likes laboratories, field work and observations, feedback and coaching.

Understanding your leaning type may give you useful information as to your ideal career direction. But whatever your preferred style, consider strengthening the under-used styles so as to become better equipped to learn from a wide range of experiences. In summary:

- Try new things, new experiences, meet new people, look for new challenges.
- Make time for reflecting on what you've learned and what it means.
- Think ahead and plan your next steps.
- Act, decide, take the risk.

Objective setting

"What do you do?" It's a common enough question when you meet someone new. The answer is usually something like "I'm a training manager" or "I work for an engineering firm".

Your job title doesn't really describe what you do at work though. It would be more accurate to say "I design training courses". But we don't want to go into detail about the actual work we do on a daily basis so we give the easy answer and leave the rest to be worked out.

Make some notes describing what you actually do. Think in terms of results rather than tasks. This is useful not only for working out your objectives but for networking - a process we address in later chapters.

What are my objectives?

Meeting objectives is part of any job. They may be part of your formal job description. Objectives describe the purpose of your job in terms of what you are expected to do or achieve.

So for example:

- Increase the frequency of the company newsletter to bi-monthly editions.
- Resolve customer queries within 48 hours of the query being raised.

Find your agreed objectives, perhaps from your job description or your last appraisal. Now compare them with the notes you made earlier describing what you do.

- What are the differences? Why are there differences?
- If what you actually do doesn't correlate with your objectives, how do you explain the discrepancy?
- Are your objectives wrong, out of date or inappropriate for a changed corporate environment? Are you doing something wrong, or are you being asked to do things that are outside the scope of or beyond your objectives?

Objectives are good for you

A lot of people don't like setting objectives. It seems bureaucratic, just more paperwork and not relevant to real life.

Clearly-written objectives are good because they give you a chance to show how well you are doing your job and where you meet or exceed your targets. They also give you a measure of control over what you do. If a task doesn't contribute to your objectives you know how to prioritise it or to refuse it. Where what you actually do doesn't correlate with your set objectives, think about the reason for that. What can you do about it? Take action.

We have already pointed out that if you have moved around a bit and worked for three or so different companies in the same sector you are more valuable to prospective employers than the person who stayed 15 years in one place.

A broad range of experience means that you have dealt with different problems and people and cultures and that adds to your employability and versatility.

If you've been in your current role 18 months or more, we guarantee you are not learning anything much new now. What do your years of experience really add up to? You need to be able to tell a career story or relate your career journey. A bit like a jigsaw puzzle, picking out the elements of your job that add up to various skills, experiences and qualifications, which taken together add up to the story of how you got to where you are now. You should be able to give several examples which demonstrate a strength in a particular skill or competence.

Now consider what skills and experience you will need for the future, for the next job along your career path. It may help to try to write a description of the best candidate for your ideal job. What would their CV look like? What are the skills and competencies needed to get that job? What shortfalls are there in your own experience?

This is at the very heart of career management – once you identify the gaps in your CV you can pursue opportunities to close them. These gaps are termed aspirational competencies. At this point, you have some thinking to do. You will have to weigh up if you would be better off staying in your existing firm in order to acquire new skills or whether it may be better to plan your next role outside the organisation.
Assuming the organisation knows and trusts you and has the appropriate headroom, they may be prepared to give you opportunities to expand your skills.

If you want to be the Sales Manager then, no matter how good a salesperson you are, you need to be working on your leadership and management skills so that you are ready to take the step up. Consider whether or not the easiest place to develop and build those skills is in your current company.

Achieving this means having an intelligent career conversation with your manager. This may not be a comfortable prospect for either of you but if you have a good relationship and can address issues and concerns, the benefits could be huge for both parties. By discussing your career plans internally, you might find there are projects on which you can work and develop the needed skills; or perhaps you can be allocated a trainee to work with you so you can start to develop management skills. Use the organisation to develop your career along the lines you want to go. If you are a good employee they should be happy to see you engaged, developing, and appreciating as an asset. This should be a win/win scenario as the organisation benefits too.

It may be that even though you are a good employee, you are very valuable where you are. Your employer may want to keep you there. Nice to know. But it doesn't help you and it's short-sighted of an employer to hold back good people for fear of losing them. If you're ambitious you're going to look elsewhere.

If you have done your homework properly and now have an idea of your career plan and the steps along the way, then you will know that this is not just about getting through to the next job. It's about the job after that too. Think about your career over the next three to five years. What do you want and where do you want to be?

Moving jobs often used to be viewed with suspicion. However, this attitude is changing and the once negative image of job-hopping has changed. Job hopping can be an attractive way to advance in times of low unemployment but a good employer values loyalty, and the best growth opportunities are often internal, particularly among those firms that recognise the morale and productivity benefits of promoting from within. Your aim is to keep learning so you need to review whether the best move is to stay with your firm or look outside.

Why don't we have proper career conversations at work?
So, there's a dilemma you have to consider when raising the issue of your career aspirations. Your employer may assume that you are looking for a new role. So be careful when approaching your boss for a career conversation. Make sure you have time scheduled for a full and frank discussion and exploration of the potential and scope for development opportunities. Even though you may think this is risky, it's important to have the conversation.

You have to weigh the possibility of changing jobs against loyalty to your company. Will your loyalty be rewarded? Are your interests aligned with those of the company and are their interests aligned with yours? What happens if your boss leaves or the company is taken over? What will your hard work and loyalty buy you then?

"Thanks for hiring me. How long will
it take you to give me a big raise
and a promotion?"

Managers don't talk often enough to their staff about career aspirations and development plans and you probably fight shy of raising the subject. It's a shame because successful career planning requires employer and employee to have mature conversations about ambitions, aspirations, potential, opportunities and growth. So pick a good time to approach your manager for a career conversation.

How to acquire your aspirational competencies
People with great careers spend time telling others about their plans and hopes. If you don't discuss the future with your manager he can't advise you or help you. Your boss may not realise you want to move into a new area of work if you don't say so.

Talk to people you admire. Talk to your role models. How did they get where they are today? What was their career path? What advice can they offer? What skills and competencies did they develop along the way? Most people like to help, they'll be flattered that you respect their opinion and happy to talk about their achievements and point you in the right direction. But if you don't ask you won't get.

Look at your network and consider it in terms of the depth of relationships and levels of influence. It goes without saying that you should aim to build strong relationships with people who have a lot of influence – use this analysis to map or segment your network so you can identify who can help you best with your career planning.

You may be reluctant to voice your aspirations and long-term career goals for fear of jeopardising your job security. Perhaps you don't want your employer to think you're dissatisfied, disloyal or planning to leave. But if that means you don't ask for training or secondments that will allow you to develop the competencies needed for your long-term career plan, then you have to leave. You have to find a role that will allow you to develop these aspirational competencies. You also have to deal with the stress and upheaval and general chaff of working your way into a new role.

It's relatively rare for people to leave jobs where they are happy, even if offered higher pay. Most people prefer stability.

The Chartered Institute of Personnel and Development's (CIPD) research shows lack of training and developmental opportunities are major reasons for staff turnover. If more organisations could get this bit right they'd improve their staff retention with the concomitant savings in recruitment costs.

If you work for a company that is good at talent management and succession planning, then management usually encourages dialogue about career paths, choices and opportunities. This sort of interaction produces a win/win situation. Employees improve their skills and competencies while the organisation benefits from an engaged and empowered workforce enabled to realise their potential as well as their ambitions. The energy, morale and commitment of the workforce are fundamental to the success of an organisation.

It has to be recognised though, that your choices and aspirations may not dovetail with those of your current manager or organisation. So you may have to think about moving laterally or taking a secondment. Think outside the box.

If you can't get the experience you need where you are, then consider filling the gaps by other means. If you need project work experience or customer contact skills, perhaps you can get this via voluntary work. You'll also enlarge your network and as you learn new skills you broaden your horizons too.

We have already looked at setting objectives. Setting yourself challenges and thinking outside of your comfort zone are good for you. Give yourself permission to do something off the wall every once in a while.

Corporate social responsibility (CSR) is a fashionable and increasingly important aspect of the modern business model. Your organisation may already have programmes set up that you can use to develop your aspirational competencies. Getting involved in these projects is good for your profile in the organisation anyway.

Exploring new environments by working on outside projects will help you to be more creative in working towards your long-term goals. You can help others while helping yourself and if your personal values are engaged too then some good must necessarily follow.

Career management rests on identification of your values, interests and skills and then building on those and investing time and effort in your career. But aim to build and grow, don't be a busy fool!

Even if you are 100% happy where you are and have no intention of moving in the near future, it's a good idea to peek over the screen of your laptop from time to time in case some interesting opportunity is in the offing.

Chances are, you'll change jobs at some point and when you get serious about finding a new role, being familiar with the market will give you an advantage. Understand your marketplace. Don't just send off CVs in scattergun fashion to inappropriate or uninterested people. Learn about the sector you are trying to break into and target your approaches.

Be proactive
Opportunities to advance don't always fall into your lap so be proactive in asking for them. To succeed you have to take charge of your career. Market yourself as a product and campaign accordingly, whether planning your next move, climbing the career ladder or reinventing your life.

There is a later chapter in this book that talks about developing a personal brand. For Tom Peters this concept encapsulates the idea that success comes from good self-packaging. This includes, but is not limited to, clothing, appearance and knowledge which lead to an indelible impression that is uniquely distinguishable. So as you think about your personal branding, consider our advice about establishing a personal brand that is authentic. Find a mentor or discuss your ideas with a few brainstorming partners and network.

Survival is about ensuring continuing appeal to employers over the long run. Do you have portable skills that will carry you through your short-term career goals and your long-term plan? Will you be able to build a portfolio of roles and interests and commitments that will constitute your third age career?

Competence isn't enough. You'll need to ensure that people who matter know who you are, and how good you are, and will want to take you with them. Think seriously about the people you know and the influence they wield - who has the potential to impact on your career? Develop a strategy that will strengthen your relationship with them. You'll also need a positive and visible profile within the organisation and to ally yourself with those who can promote your career. It's about being well connected and making sure your contribution is noticed. Do make sure, though, that you are known for all the right reasons – going the extra mile; reliability and getting things done; bright ideas. As opposed to wrong reasons – the person who got silly at the Christmas party.

How can you raise your profile and credibility within the organisation? If you want a solid career it's essential to develop and exhibit good leadership skills, so think about those CSR and volunteer projects. They can help you build skills and contacts and they look good on your CV.

Taking charge of your own career is an imperative for success in the fast moving, modern business environment. Which skills do you need to make yourself more marketable? Consider yourself as a product and campaign accordingly, whether planning your next move, climbing the career ladder or reinventing your life. Be sure your personal branding is congruent with your ideals and ambitions. Seek out every relevant opportunity for continuous learning and professional development. Do you need a new qualification, to learn Mandarin Chinese, or some coaching in leadership skills? Look for a competitive advantage. What are other professionals in your field offering? Can you differentiate yourself by offering something extra, different or unique?

Cross-reference your competitive advantage with the ideal candidate for your ideal job. If you are an appreciating asset you have hit on the secret of employability. The danger in staying somewhere too long, is that only in the first 18 months in a role are you learning and growing in value as an employee. Time spent doing the same things is time when you are not appreciating in value. So keep your Career MOT in mind and review it regularly to ensure you are staying on track.

When the marketplace is changing fast you need to stay ahead of the game. You may become obsolete if you don't keep up.

It's not an age thing
People ask "Will my age count against me?" "Am I too old?" You can't teach an old dog new tricks! Somewhat tongue in cheek, I say there is no such thing as age discrimination.

If you have skills, say as an analyst or a Java programmer, and you are 64 years old you can get a job tomorrow. If, on the other hand, you are a 32 year old and have been working in VHS Video production and that is all you can do, then you are dispensable. You had better start learning some new tricks quickly.

The problem with age, and we're generalising here, is that the older we get the less we self-invest. So if you have learned no new skills or have gained no new understanding of your business or your specialty in the last 6 months then you are well on the road to obsolescence and beckoning unemployment.

Continuing professional development is not just something your professional association or the HR department talk about for the fun of it. If you don't keep up with the game someone else will be brought in to take your place. That's why it's important to make an effort to work in a variety of organisations and multi-cultural environments if you can.

Creativity, the ability to look at problems from different angles, to think laterally is something to cultivate. Don't assume the old way of working is still the best. "We've always done it that way" is simply not good enough.

The benefit of seeing something from a different angle was beautifully demonstrated by an iconic advertisement for the Guardian Newspaper on television. The scene opens where, at first sight, you watch a young man, looking like a skinhead wearing combats and boots, turn and run towards a man walking down the street holding a briefcase.

The man turns and they appear to grapple with the case on the pavement alongside a construction site. The assumption is clear; he looks like a mugger. However as the camera angle changes, you can see the man with the briefcase is about to be hit by something falling from overhead. The young man is trying to pull him into the safety of a doorway. He is, in fact, a hero. Meanwhile we have all been taught a valuable lesson.

Guardian Advert: Points of View 1986
(http://www.youtube.com/ watch?v=E3h-T3KQNxU)

Don't make assumptions and do consider all possible options! You can see this for yourself on YouTube if you search for 'Guardian Advert - Points of View'. There is an updated version concerning diverse public opinion and the case of the Three Little Pigs and The Big Bad Wolf. The message is the same: Get the whole picture.

So learning to think around things from an array of perspectives is a valuable skill. Working in new environments, problem solving, working overseas, expanding your horizons, breaking out of your comfort zone or taking a secondment will help develop learning agility. This reinforces my point that working for competitors is a good thing, you get different management skills from working in different environments.

If you work for an investment bank then try to spend time working in the public sector, for instance, understanding the problems of the homeless by helping a charity or CSR project. Racehorses are blinkered to keep them on track and stop them being distracted. A blinkered attitude towards work and life means you miss the big picture and the endless possibilities out there.

No matter where your start point was, any career can lose its charm over time. For example, let's imagine that at the outset a career in investment banking seemed like an interesting and tough challenge, alongside the thrill of making money. However, if you've been successful and now have money in the bank, that initial drive may wane. Perhaps it's not as much fun as it used to be getting up at dawn in order to be ready when the markets open. It's not so unusual these days for people in their forties or fifties to consider a completely different second career.

Whole new perspectives open up when you open your eyes to what's beyond the boundaries of the world you have always worked in.

Don't let your career just happen and don't wait to be noticed. Take a proactive, targeted approach to maximise your potential and you'll get more fulfillment from its challenges. You are responsible for your own future.

There's more to life than work. But as the world of work changes it's sometimes hard to make time to spend on family and other interests, to satisfy emotional and spiritual needs, as well as earning a crust.

This is a holistic view of personal development: don't just learn for the sake of your job but for the sake of your life. Develop curiosity. Learn to question more. In a changing world the ability to adapt is going to be increasingly important.

Be generous. Take every opportunity you can to thank people, to include them in what you are doing. And help them where you can.

In summary:

- Look at and objectively assess your strengths and competencies.
- Play to your strengths.
- Actively seek out learning opportunities - be open to new ideas and challenges.

Chapter 3

Understanding yourself and planning your career

"There are three things that are extremely hard: steel, a diamond and to know one's self."

Benjamin Franklin

What this chapter tells you about Everlasting Employability. The importance of:

- Visualising the future 3 to 5 years out.
- Identifying your ideal job
- Determining what the very best candidate needs for a particular role.
- Assessing yourself against the very best candidate today.
- Getting a mentor.
- How the perversity of recruitment stops you getting your ideal job.

This book is designed to help you work things out for yourself. There are no right answers. If you were looking for "Twelve Steps to a Perfect Career" then you're going to be disappointed. You have to take the time to review and reflect.

Ask yourself – does what you choose to do on a daily basis give you the satisfaction you really want? If not, then how are you going to achieve it?

A driver, hopelessly off course, pulls up near a local man and asks for directions. The rustic looks up the road, then down the road, back up the road and thinks for a bit, and then says: "Well I wouldn't start from here".

It's an old joke but the point is that you can only start from where you are right now. You have to work with what you've got.

We want to help you get your next job but more importantly We want to help you plan and map your career and future.

Where do you start?
Start gathering information; take stock and observe what's really going on – with your life, with your career, with your world.

"We need to do a better job
of fooling ourselves."

Take the time to be aware of what you are feeling – are you happy, are you satisfied with your job, your career, your place in life? Tune in to what matters to you so that you can work with that. You're the only one who can decide what you want your life to look like.

Here are some helpful questions to ask yourself:

- Am I getting better at what I do?
- Am I doing what I love in the right way?
- Does what I do really mean something to me, do I care about it?
- Is it real and honest and is it what I meant to do?

Taking control

How do you plan in an age of uncertainty?

Organisations have to change to grow but in order to achieve their objectives, even with consultation, they tend to impose change and then are surprised when they encounter resistance. Take a really good look at the change situation you are facing and figure out exactly what you can achieve in the new environment. Ideally the new scenario should be of mutual benefit. There may be new opportunities to learn new skills. Consider what you can and cannot control. Don't waste energy and resources on what you can't control, focus on what you can manage.

At this point, I'd like to stress again that your career is not the responsibility of the organisation you work for. Some excellent employers may think about the continued employability of their employees. but it's not safe to assume that this will always be the case. Your career direction and the organisation's objectives may diverge at any time so be very clear; you should use the organisation to achieve your goals and not vice versa.

The worst mistake you can make is to bequeath the management of your career to the organisation and we use word "bequeath" in the direst possible sense.

So visualise pressing the fast forward button on your life and imagine yourself into the future. As a bonus, you can design your ideal job.

In your time-traveller vision of the future you are not constrained by anything. Imagine what's on your desk? Who are your clients? What can you see from your office window? Allow your imagination to run wild. Picture how you spent yesterday in this ideal role. Build a job description.

When you picture yourself in the future think about how that envisioning of success makes you feel.

Case study

I worked with a lady called Leann who had been made redundant from a city bank. We talked about her options and her approach to finding a new role but she couldn't work up much enthusiasm for the search. Going back into the fray just didn't look enticing.

I asked her what she wanted to do. "All bets are off. You can do whatever you want. Be whatever you want. What does that look like?" Straight back at me, without hesitation, she said "I'd love to run my own art gallery". Now we were getting somewhere. "So what's stopping you?" I asked her.

Leann set up and ran a small gallery which represents young emerging talent in the world of modern art. The business idea was to lease paintings to employers to significantly improve the working environment whilst taking a monthly fee rather than a one-off payment. This provided the artists with an income. Whilst Leann did not make vast amounts of money from this venture, she did find a career that engaged her passion for modern art.

Take time. Do justice to yourself. What is stopping you from doing what you want?

So for successful career planning and management you need to

- visualise where you want to be in 3 to 5 years time,
- decide what your ideal job looks like,
- articulate what you need to be to be the very best candidate for that job and write it down!

As Aleksandr Orlov, the meerkat, would say – "Simples!"

Now imagine yourself as the person to whom you report in this ideal job. You have to recruit the very best candidate. What skills, knowledge, qualifications and expertise does the very best candidate need?

1. Write down the ideal job description and the job specification for the very best possible candidate.
2. What qualifications, experience, skills and competencies is the hiring manager looking for? Label these – A for Essential, B for Desirable and C for Peripheral.
3. Rate them out of 10 to establish priority ranking.

There's a spreadsheet plan in the Appendix that you can use as a matrix for the visualisation exercise described above.

Now you have a specification for your ideal job. Return to today. Rewind.

Rate yourself out of 10 against those criteria and establish the gap between the very best candidate and your current level of performance.

It's really useful to get a third party to help you with this, someone you trust to help you with rating. Remember it is against the very best candidate that you are measuring yourself. When you ask them to rate you tell them to be frank. It's important to be realistic.

If there are two or more areas where there is a gap of more than 2 then you can't get that job today.

If there is only one area with a gap you can get that job today; so go to the chapters on networking and then preparing for interview. These chapters show you how to set about getting that job.

You'll need to persevere with this exercise and it's worth getting someone you trust to help – mentor, career coach, or partner. Someone who you can bounce ideas off and who will help keep you motivated. Sharing ideas and experiences can help you make sense of what's going on around you and encourage you to try new things.

Depending on where you are in your career you are going to need different mentors for different circumstances. If you are looking for a career change or dealing with redundancy you need to pick someone who can help you deal with that.

If you really can't visualise the ideal job, what then? This is where a mentor or career coach can really help you take stock.

The Career MOT is your starting point for an overhaul of your career plan and a plan for the route ahead.

The importance of the rating-yourself exercise is not so much to identify your next job as to establish the gaps in your skills and experience that you need to eradicate in order to get the dream job.
However good a salesman you are, if you want a sales management role you'll need some supervisory experience. What we're recommending is a stepping stone approach.

You have to drive your career forward, so once you have identified your skills gap you need to work on eradicating the gap. Don't take another job that leaves you with the same gap in experience. That's the road to obsolescence.

The great perversity of recruitment is that you only get hired for the skills, knowledge and expertise you already have. So at the outset we have a Catch-22 situation - how do you develop those aspirational skills, how do you close the gaps in your experience?

It's important to be aware of the skills, qualifications and experience you need to close the aspirational competency gap. You need to put in place a plan which you should discuss with your career mentor and selected members of your network. Find people who already have those competencies and how they achieved them. Take time to research – there's a wealth of information out there.

The easiest place to improve your skills and experience is with your current employer if those opportunities are within reach. That's why intelligent career conversations at work are so important, as we highlighted in the previous chapter. You can decide whether it's best to stay or to move on to your next role outside the organisation.

Better the devil you know or better to move on?

Chapter 4

How to build the career of your dreams

"Success is not the key to happiness. Happiness is the key to success. If you love what you are doing, you will be successful."

Albert Schweitzer

What this chapter tells you about Everlasting Employability:

- Managing your career is down to you.
- Having a diversity of roles in a range of organisations is important.
- Seeing change as an opportunity.
- Writing down your goals.
- Sharing your hopes and aspirations.
- The power of visualisation.
- Career planning as a skill you can learn.

As we have already discussed, the job for life is a rarity. Modernisation of the world of work and the cut-throat battle for talent in all sectors means that staying put is often no longer an option. Nobody with employable skills need be unemployed. Nobody is unemployable. You can get a job if you want to if you focus, research, plan, network and persist. Harness your creativity and cultivate a willingness to examine and assess your career and your career progress.

We know, and you know, that your career is down to you. Don't sub-contract it. It is not the job of a recruitment agency or a headhunter to plan your career path and pick jobs that get you to your goal.

Case study

Paul was made redundant from an agrochemical company. He was well qualified and had good experience but he looked around and didn't like the idea of staying in agrochemicals as a chemist.

He and his wife bought a smallholding. Then they bought some llamas. It was hard work, cold in the winter and a struggle to make ends meet at first. Now their llamas win prizes at agricultural shows and they run a thriving business and the llama wool is used to make wonderful and very expensive shawls and throws. It's not the 9 to 5 routine and farming is no soft option but Paul is never going back to an office job now.

So don't believe the organisation you work for if they tell you that they are going to manage your career for you. Some firms do have talent management programmes and processes but ultimately you have to plough your own furrow.

Travel broadens the mind. It's the same with our careers. A diversity of roles and companies enable you to build a CV that sells you as a top flight commodity. The right spread of skills and depth of experience are what will carry you through to success in your chosen field. This applies whether you want to achieve a chief executive role with a multi-million pound quoted company or just a more senior role in the supermarket where you work three days a week to supplement your income from writing or painting or teaching yoga.

Realistically your aspirations have to be backed by the right skills and experience, not just pipe dreams. If that means you have to pay for training or take a secondment to a foreign office, you have to weigh the costs against the potential benefits.

A wide range of challenges and experience makes us more versatile and attractive as potential employees. This is partly because we learn most in new environments as we learn to apply our skills and knowledge to them. We learn from working in a new culture or within a different business model. We learn from change and as we adapt and adjust we should grow in confidence. A judicious mix of roles and skills is going to reflect well in your CV.

It's unrealistic to expect a career for life. It's not impossible, but the speed of technological advance and your personal development over a 30 year working lifespan militates against a one-track career.

Most people let their careers just happen, they fall into jobs that are offered and stay because they don't focus on what really matters and what will get them where they want to be. Most people spend more time planning their next holiday or choosing an iPad than they spend thinking about their next career move.

That sort of reactive approach is too passive. If you only respond to external stimuli and never take a chance, you won't make the sort of changes this book is about or build a career that will be fulfilling and rewarding.

How to help yourself
Change is hard. Most people are wary of change, even afraid of it, and worry about it more than they need to.

Try to see change as an opportunity. Look for the good in the changing situation. Only worry about the things that you can control, not what you can't control. You have to work with the change because you can't work against it!

Nothing lasts forever. Things are going to change one way or another, whether you like it or not. What you need to cultivate is the ability to find ways to gain advantages from change, to work out how to exploit the possibilities of your changing environment.

You have to learn to be a change expert. Damian Hughes, one of our favourite business writers, refers to "liquid thinking" and says that those who thrive on change are those who see and plan ahead.

Try not to dwell on shock or anger when things don't go your way or when events overtake you. Face the situation and work out what you can take from it that will make you stronger and better placed to face the challenges presented to you by redundancy, takeover, divorce, bankruptcy or failure to get the second interview. If you can build the skills and attitude to deal with change then you will have gained something positive. Everyone can spring back from a major change but it takes time to adjust and that time period is different for individuals based on a number of factors. These can include how much warning you have had of the impending change and how much you may have been able to think through your options and get comfortable with them.

You may have read of the change curve researched by Kubler Ross which identifies the distinct phases involved in adjusting to a change. There is the initial shock where you can't quite believe what has happened, followed by a brief sense of optimism. But as reality sets in there can be an unproductive downward spiral as you struggle to adjust. Finally, as light starts to dawn, the final phase is acceptance. More detail on the change curve is provided later in Chapter 13.

Changing the way you work, manage, deliver or do things is hard too. Psychologists say it takes at least 21 days to change, or indeed to develop, a habit.

Dr Maxwell Maltz found that the human mind takes almost exactly 21 days to start to adjust to a major life change, whether it's negative like the loss of a limb, a change of employment or residence, or positive like embarking on a new romantic relationship. Dr Maltz has written a number of books that deal with this subject, including *Creative Living for Today, The Magical Power of Self-Image Psychology* and the bestseller *Psycho-Cybernetics*, which has achieved sales of more that 30 million copies.

Those of you who are ex-smokers know it can be hard to stick with the decision to change, sometimes after much longer than three weeks have gone by. Blame your neural pathways for habits that form and become life-long. Brain circuits take engrams (memory traces) and produce neuro-connections and neuro-pathways only if they are bombarded for 21 days in a row. But 21 days repetition of a new behaviour means you will win through to your desired behaviour becoming a habit or breaking the bad habit.

Remember that change happens because of a single decision - a single moment, your decision to make the change. To deal effectively with change you need to focus on success.

Most self-help books will suggest you write down your goals and plans. Thomas Schelling of Harvard University looked at the ways in which we enforce rules on ourselves and recommends the "write-it-down" technique for two reasons:

> One is precision: writing invites careful formulation of boundaries, exceptions, penalties and rewards. The other is ceremony: formalising the rule in writing, perhaps with witnesses, attaches moral authority and makes violation more threatening to one's integrity, raising the stakes.

Put simply, writing things down makes you think through what you mean. Also you are more likely to do it if you have written it down, because the very act of writing is the first step to commitment.

Schelling was thinking in terms of giving up smoking or persisting with diet and exercise plans, but it works for other change programmes too.

I'm a list person. If you write it down then you're making a commitment. You are more likely to do something about your goals than otherwise. Seeing your plan in black and white is a powerful motivator. Ticking things off your plan as they are achieved helps you maintain forward momentum.

I like to tick-off achievements from the To Do List so much that on occasions I have written down a task just for the satisfaction of ticking it off again. There is pleasure in acknowledging progress.

To make successful changes to the ways you do things you'll need patience, persistence, support, resilience and bags of determination.

Share your hopes and aspirations
Telling people about your aspirations helps because enlisting the support and encouragement of others bolsters your commitment and your confidence. You will not achieve your career goals without help; you need a network as they are your eyes and ears. The more people there are in your network and the more they know about your goals, the more likely they are to help you. And the more likely you are to succeed.

Revisiting your list after you've been working on your plans for a while is interesting too. I have a holiday book in which I write down my hopes and aspirations. I always revisit the book twelve months later on the next holiday to review how things turned out, what I achieved and so on.

As we change and grow, the original plan may have to be reconsidered and amended. You may find you have branched out into new areas of interest and ambition that have opened up as you have been working towards your goal. Be open to change and exploration and alternatives.

Try to associate with people who understand and appreciate you and those who like your work. Not everybody will like you - that's highly unlikely - but nurture those who make you feel good. Be positive and share your enthusiasms. We are all unique and uniquely talented.

If you want something badly enough, you can usually find a way to get it if you are prepared to plan, invest and qualify yourself for the opportunity of a lifetime. I know an outplacement client with a passion for football who now works as a football statistician.

Making a career transition is not easy and you may have to forego financial security and the comforts of the corporate world but only you can weigh up what really matters to you.

Edgar Schein developed a theory on what he called Career Anchors. Through a series of questions you can deduce what it is that drives you and gives satisfaction. Is it the pure challenge, entrepreneurship or money that motivates you? How important is job security or being of service to others or being respected as a technical expert? Knowing what makes you tick is all important in career choice.

Visualising the Big Picture
The other thing you need to do is think big. Visualise success, don't sweat the small stuff, think big picture. It's OK to fantasise. Look back to the David Beckham story I quoted earlier. See that goal with your mind's eye; hear the noise as the stadium goes wild.

"Someone who says they saw a
'Now Hiring' sign in front of
our building in a dream last
night is here to see you."

Where would you like to be? What do you really want to be doing in five years' time? The more you can visualise what you really want from life, the more granular that visualisation is, the easier it is to set your target in your sights and head in the right direction.

It's not really about job titles. You might aim to be the CFO of a listed company by the year 2015, but it's actually about the reality of working life.

So what will your office look like? What will you do in your working day? Are you seeing clients? Selling new products? Inventing new processes? In the perfect job what does tomorrow look like? This micro-visualisation is important as part of the process. It lets you imagine what your perfect career looks like. We forget how to use make-believe as we get older. The issue here is to take the fantasy and understand what it is that you need to get there.

If you can imagine the perfect job then you can start the process of imagining the best candidate for that job.

Career management requires you to tap into your creativity and dream as well as analyse yourself. If your strategy to fund your retirement is to buy a weekly lottery ticket, then read no further. If, however, you believe it's not a case of luck, but of having a well executed, simple long-term plan, read on.

There is always an opportunity, even in challenging market conditions, to think positively and creatively. You need to build a personal strategy to identify and access the hidden job market – i.e. the jobs that are not advertised or handled by agencies. It is estimated that only around 20% of jobs are advertised which leaves 80% that are filled through networks. This means there are jobs out there that are right for you.

Talented people are in demand, more than ever before. Yes, there's an ocean of CVs sloshing around out there but the talented few are the ones in demand. Ask anybody running a business and they'll tell you that the most difficult challenge they face is finding good people.

Think of Jose Mourinho, regarded by some as one of the best football coaches of all time or the "special one" – that's how he refers to himself. It's a little bit arrogant, but he's a top manager and he says so. He has built his profile and staked his reputation on the performance of his teams. Because he lives up to his self-declared reputation, he can get away with it. So build your profile and your reputation with the aim of becoming the best candidate you can imagine for the role you want.

The world is changing fast and in ways that are hard to imagine. You need to be one step ahead. Things today that we take for granted, such as the smartphone, we could not have visualised ten years ago. When planning your career that's part of the challenge. We can't possibly know what lies ahead.

The proactive career plan is about maintaining your appeal to employers over the long run. Competence isn't enough. You need to ensure that people who matter know who you are, how good you are and want to take you with them. You also need a positive and visible profile and to ally yourself with those who can promote your career. To be effective you'll need to be a good networker and this is such an important skill that there's a whole chapter dedicated to this later in the book. However, when you're networking remember that it's good to spend time with your friends and contacts too - don't forget that it's supposed to be fun.

If your skills are in short supply you'll be paid a premium, but remember you will need 30 plus years of employability so you can't afford to rest on your laurels. If ten years ago you decided you wanted a career as a telex operator, you made the wrong choice. But if you're a website developer you may be on a roll by now.

This book is less about how you perform at interview than about taking a long-term perspective and changing your behaviour so that you are in demand and ready to step up when you find an opportunity you don't want to pass up.

This is not a book about how to write a CV. Our overview of career books suggests that most focus on the CV; this is not one of them. In fact, there is a chapter about writing a CV but only because I thought you'd be disappointed if it wasn't there and I've helped write a lot of them for clients. Producing a CV is simply part of the broader question of how to market yourself effectively.

Although work is about sustenance it should also be about nourishment and flourishing. If you can do what you love you're really lucky. Live your values. It should be fun and all this should be conveyed in how you portray yourself.

Most people don't like planning. It's easier to procrastinate and let things take their course. The danger is that, if you don't make some realistic plans, you will be overtaken by events and your options will contract.

If you just stand in the middle of the road waiting to see what happens then you're going to get hit by a big truck sometime soon.

The most important person in the proactive career planning process is the person reading this book.

Now let's get on with it.

Chapter 5

Investing in yourself

"In oneself lies the whole world and if you know how to look and learn then the door is there and the key is in your hand. Nobody on earth can give you either the key or the door to open, except yourself."

J. Krishnamurti

What this chapter tells you about Everlasting Employability:

- Careers last a long time and you need to remain current.
- The importance of having a personal brand.
- How people take in information.
- How to be remembered for the right things.
- Why mentors are essential.

If you need a career rethink, then consider what's most important to you. The list might be: intellectual stimulation, time for family, using existing skills, developing new skills, variety, people contact, autonomy, a consultative culture or empowering manager. Build a personal development plan focussed on what you find rewarding and stimulating and put yourself in charge of your future.

I've put a template for a personal development plan in the Appendix so you can plot out your objectives and how to achieve them and visualise what you think success will look like.

I'm a football fan so here's another football anecdote. David Beckham is shown in a home video, taken when he was around 10 years old, telling the cameraman how he dreams of becoming a professional footballer.

David was born and brought up in London but which football strip do you suppose he was wearing in this old film? Manchester United, of course!

From an early age he dreamt of just one thing - becoming a great player for Manchester United.

So, you need to visualise and plan your career, but crucially you need to invest in it. The perfect career won't just happen; you are responsible for your own destiny. If you spend more time planning your social life than you spend planning your next career move you could find yourself stuck in a rut.

You need to understand each phase of your career strategy and be clear about what is important to you. Ensure your personal values are aligned with your work and other commitments or you will lose interest in your job pretty quickly.

If you can plot out a career plan then you know you have to invest in yourself in order to succeed. Look at your role models, what do they do? How do they keep up to date, stay in touch with new developments?

One of the things I've talked about is ensuring your long-term employability. You need to be PC literate; you need to be well informed. Just scanning the paper probably is not enough. Keep up to date with your field and with developments in management thinking and new business practices. The Harvard Business Review and McKinsey Quarterly make good general business reading and read the specialist press for your area of expertise. Be alert to the possibilities around you; apply some lateral thinking and grow your knowledge and insights into areas around and beyond your own area of expertise.

Hand on heart – can you achieve your ambitions from where you are currently? Do you need to think seriously about formal education, qualifications, continuing professional development programmes? The pursuit of knowledge and self-knowledge are all grist to the mill. You need to differentiate yourself from the crowd.

Climbing the corporate ladder is not achieved without a great deal of hard work. You can't expect opportunities to come to you. You have to find them or make them and keep your skills refreshed and up to date so that when a potential role crops up you look like the ideal candidate.

If you could learn anything what would it be? A language, an instrument, a skill or a craft or a science? What does this tell you? What would be different for you if you could learn to play the flute or tile the bathroom walls or speak Russian?

If you have the cash, time and commitment to achieve an MBA, will it make the difference you are looking for?

How could you learn to do these things? Research them. You don't have to change career. Learn Russian anyway, just because you are interested in it. Learning it will do you good, stimulate the mind and will enrich your life, even if you never do get a job with a Russian company.

My co-author, Linda Jackson, likes to point out that it's a good job we learn to walk when we're very young. Given that it takes a year of sustained effort, most of us would give up if we tried to learn to walk in our 20s or 30s. All too often we lack self-belief. That inner voice would be telling us that we weren't cut out for such athleticism! The reality is that it's amazing what you can do with enough determination. After all, we all learned to walk. It could be useful to remind ourselves that we all possess grit and determination and the tenacity to succeed, if we want something badly enough.

Well, you might say that you have not enough time. Or no money. Or no talent. Why limit yourself like that?

Discard self-limiting beliefs. Inspiration comes to the inspired and momentum comes when we discard inertia. You know that you can make the time, get up half an hour earlier, use your lunch break or forego the television a couple of evenings a week. Learning new things is good for us in many ways and changing the way we do things, from time to time, is good too.

Look again at the chapter on Understanding Yourself and revisit your self-imposed limitations. Don't beat yourself up for wanting to be what you really are. If you understand your values and motivations and see the patterns you work in then you can knock the self-defeating stuff on the head and take action.

Personal brand

Personal branding is about how you package your strengths, talents, values and beliefs. It is about how you present them to others so they understand what makes you identifiable, unique and makes you stand out from the crowd.

What do you want others to say about you? Is it reflected in how you look, sound and behave? Your brand needs to evolve with your environment, culture, career and life aspirations.

Research shows that over 93% of first impressions are based on how we present ourselves. Of that, only 55% is based on our image and how we visually appear others.   It's not just about the clothes you wear. We therefore need to ensure that we make an instant positive impact.

This is important because it's about seeing yourself as a product. Managing what is recognisable about you. Think about what you stand for from the perspective of what the other guy sees. How are you perceived by your peers, colleagues, suppliers, customers and friends?

What will people remember about you? What do you want them to remember?

"I hope you don't have an irrational
bias against job candidates who
wear tie-dye suits."

Don't forget the importance of Twitter for your personal brand. If you're trying to build a strong personal brand, then focus your Twitter handle, avatar and bio information to align with your personal brand and LinkedIn profile. There is more detailed information on how to do this later in the book in chapter 8.

So how would you describe your own personal impact? What are your USP's (unique selling points)? For example, you might say approachable, dynamic and knowledgeable. The word 'professional' should be a given.

How do others describe your personal impact? In other words, how are you marketing yourself? Remember most of the information we process is visual but don't forget your written brand. How you look on LinkedIn for example, your networked self.

Visual impact - not just how you dress but your body language - is a key part of your communication armoury. So how do you package your strengths, talents, values and beliefs? Is that packaging congruent with what you stand for and reflected in how you look, sound and behave? This branding and how you present yourself to others are what make you memorable.

The actual content of what we say accounts for just 7% of what we communicate – so how you look, how you sound, and your body language say a lot about you. You need to ensure that you make an instant and positive impact.

There is a real need for self-awareness here and for ensuring your behaviour is consistent with your brand values. If you say you are meticulous, don't hand out a CV with typos in it. If you claim to be reliable, don't turn up late for meetings.

Your brand is how you project yourself to the world. Decide what to say or write in order to convey a certain image. Your projected image influences what others think of you and how they might choose to interact with you.

Awareness of what others see will help you to identify blind spots and deal with practical problems or self-projection.

Research shows that you have up to five seconds to make that instant impact. Think about these questions:

1. What do you want people to say about you?
2. What do people perceive when you walk into a room?
3. Is your brand current and representative of your future aspirations?

If you described yourself as an excellent communicator, competent, and detail orientated - does this dovetail with how you look, sound and behave? Is there a stain on that tie or a button missing from your cuff or any fraying on the bottom of those trousers? If you are late, can you explain fluently, convincingly and charmingly why you were late?

It's not just about image. A good hair cut and clean shoes are essential. That's a given. Neither does anyone want to shake hands with someone whose hands and nails look like they've just finished servicing a motorbike or spent copious amounts of time digging the garden. A spiffy suit and new shirt all help but a superficial image that doesn't reflect your individuality and personality will be transparent and obviously inauthentic. Start by understanding exactly who you are, what you're capable of, where you want to go. Make sure that it's the real deal; build a stable brand to exhibit your trustworthiness, credibility, and personal charisma. This way you will feel so much more confident and relaxed.

So now define your attributes and ambitions into a statement of what you want your visible brand to be. Work on a personal brand statement. Then actively engage in living up to that statement and showing off your brand. It's common sense but if it's authentic then it will boost your confidence.

Self-esteem is about how you see yourself and personal branding is about how others see you. Think about what you want people to say about you when you leave the room.

Your personal brand is reflected in what people say about you after they meet you. But don't just concentrate on first impressions. What about the lasting impression you make on others?

What is your "MacGuffin"? In other words, what is about you that catches the attention of others? Justin Urquhart Stewart has his trademark red braces; John McCririck has his hat; Boris Johnson has his haircut. It doesn't have to be something so outrageous but distinctive – just something people will remember when they see you again.

It doesn't even have to be that extraordinary but it has to leave a positive impression. So be positive, be cheerful, competent, effective, polite, work the charm, be nice to know. Negativity is not the image you want to leave behind. When you are working on your personal brand the input of a mentor can be invaluable.

Working with a mentor

For the avoidance of doubt, we should explain that a mentor is someone credible whom you trust and who can help you develop. Typically he or she may be someone in your industry who has more experience than you, someone more senior who might be a suitable role model and someone who you feel at ease with and can be honest with about the advice you seek. You should have different mentors at different stages in your career to help you with particular aspects of your life.

Why is a mentor important? Successful people seek feedback. Being reflective is a key component for the proactive job search. Using a mentor allows you to leverage off the expertise of someone who has been there, done that and understands the space.

A mentoring relationship is not for life. You agree upfront what you want to achieve and how you will work together. Formulate a two way contract that suits you both. This could be to help you set strategic achievable objectives in a new role but would also include how often you expect to meet so that expectations are set.

The first thing to remember is that mentoring is not a cure-all for every problem and decision facing the mentee. Mentors aren't there to do your work for you; rather they exist to guide, support and help you develop the skills you already have. Like all good partnerships, it's about working together. If you are a mentee you need to be honest with yourself and your mentor about what you want to achieve.

To make it work well you need to cultivate a degree of objectivity and resilience that allows you put to good use the advice you get from your mentor, even when it is hard work.

A good mentor forces personal review, even if it hurts. Often when we seek advice, what we are actually doing is looking for validation of what we have already decided. Sometimes we just need someone to bounce ideas off, and a mentor can help identify options and alternatives.

A mentor needs to be flexible, able and willing to offer practical guidance in respect of specific problems where requested - but most importantly of all be ready to encourage the mentee to make the actual decision and move forward.

The way the relationship operates will depend on the needs and experience of both parties and the degree of commitment a mentor is able to make. The mentor should make it clear what support it is possible to provide and neither party should be afraid to set clear maximum time commitments. After all, stretching your time too thinly is a major cause of issues in personal relationships.

Mentees should respect their mentor's time by agreeing to schedule another meeting to discuss topics that remain at the end of the session – rather than presuming their needs take priority. At the conclusion of a meeting, summarise agreements made. Restate what you will be doing and what your mentor has agreed to do for you. This way the relationship will keep on track.

In summary, remember mentors are not instant friends. Whilst being friendly may be a healthy attribute in a business relationship, it's sensible to remember that mentors are not the same as friends. Your relationship with one is usually confined to professional matters. A mentor is a sage who will share their wisdom with you and on occasion will need to be brutally honest in their feedback.

Chapter 6

Why people fail to get the jobs they want

"The most beautiful fate, the most wonderful good fortune that can happen to any human being, is to be paid for doing that which he passionately loves to do."

Abraham H. Maslow

What this chapter tells you about Everlasting Employability:

. How to avoid the most common mistakes that people make when job searching.

People fail for a whole host of reasons. Some seem blindingly obvious and sometimes, for no obvious reason, things just don't work out the way you'd like.

Applying for the wrong job

We see an advert and think we can do 70% of what the job description lists and we'd like to do it. So we fool ourselves that we can write a CV or an application that makes us the ideal candidate. But really there is no point in applying unless you are at least a 95% match in today's market – otherwise there will be far better qualified candidates than you.

A national advertisement or online advertisement can generate between 50 and 250 respondents. The recruiter will very quickly make three piles – exact matches, possible matches and no-hopers. If you don't rate a match of something like 90%+ you don't get into the exact match heap.

You can be almost certain that an advert will produce between 10 or 15 exact matches. So the other 235 candidates are wasting their time, as their application is only skim-read. That's not to say that you can't talk your way in to a job for which you are not 100% qualified, but you have to do it through networking. Approaching it through an advertisement or online ad won't work. So use the proactive job search model in Chapter 7.

Failure to use networking

You need a sponsor. Going into any organisation where you are an unknown commodity puts you at a disadvantage. Spending your time cold calling or emailing or sending in responses to job advertisements that you are not a match for is not productive. And you can kid yourself that you are being busy. When I hear on late night radio shows people saying they can't get a job despite writing 300 letters, I think that's just not a good use of time.

Wrong mind-set

You need to maintain a positive psychological attitude – if you go in to an interview thinking you won't get the job then it will be no surprise when you don't get it. If you have little confidence you can do the job, why should an employer take the risk? Those who believe they will be successful will land the role they want while those who don't, won't.

Just bubbling under the wrong mindset is **lack of resilience**. Most people give up too easily. They fail to make connections and they don't network because it's too difficult. The proactive job search is not for the fainthearted. But after all it is your career and your livelihood so you owe it to yourself to make the push.

Failure to prepare for the interview

The key thing is practice, practice, practice. If you can do a video-taped practice interview and watch it back, that can be a big help. Gary Player said *"the more I practise, the luckier I get."* So learn your lines and refer to Chapter 10 for more tips on interview skills.

Sub-contracting the job search to a third party

Don't expect an agency or headhunter to do all the work. This is particularly true for middle to senior executives who tend to think they are going to get a job the same way they did when they were in their early

20s. Then you were a commodity and only had to send out CVs and if your skills were in short supply you got an interview. But the market has changed and your pride will be severely dented if you think the same approach will work for you now. Many headhunters will not have the time or inclination to call you back and follow up if you are not the perfect candidate for a role they are trying to fill. Let's think about this for a moment – who is the best person to represent you? What is going to impress an employer more – you calling them following a recommendation or someone else trying to sell you for a commission? Even for more senior level appointments the rules of the game have changed.

You fail to invest in yourself

You haven't developed an employable skill set. Again this is more prevalent among senior executives who fool themselves by saying "I've have had lots of jobs in the same company." That may be true but it doesn't give you a varied skill set. The longer we stay in the same environment the more institutionalised we become. Employers want candidates who understand what it is like to work in different environments, not just one firm.

You don't have a career plan

If you haven't invested in yourself then you probably don't have a career plan either. You are likely to be less impressive as a candidate because you can't tell people definitively where you are heading.

You don't know when to quit

Do the same things all the time and you will get the same results. You can have too much resilience – chasing the same job, in the same sector. It will be a waste of time if the marketplace no longer wants those skills. Cut your losses quickly, recognise that your job search would be best served by looking elsewhere.

Things you are powerless to change

There are some things you cannot change and cannot control, such as deeply ingrained personality traits which can affect an individual's leadership style and actions. When under pressure, most people will display certain counterproductive tendencies. Under normal circumstances these characteristics may actually be strengths. For example, someone who is detail conscious may start to feel stress when the volume of work starts to increase. Someone who likes to think in quiet space may become edgy if forced to work in a noisy open plan office.

You don't think you have any options

If you are constrained by financial considerations, children, mortgage, etc. then don't just sit there hoping for the best. That's the worst thing you can do. There are things you can control but you have to take control; there is no such thing as having no options. When we work with people in an outplacement setting they often find themselves surprised at how many options they have when they really start to think about it. Humans get stuck in comfort zones. We tell ourselves that we have no options but really we aren't trying hard enough. The longevity of mankind is down to adaptability and dealing with change.

Case study

I once worked with a very successful senior banker in his mid-forties. Over the years he had managed to squirrel away a nice little nest egg to just about keep him and his family in the style to which they'd become accustomed. Lucky them! There was just one problem - he was bored rigid and beginning to get depressed. His values had changed and he now wanted something new to challenge him - something entrepreneurial. As luck would have it, an ideal opportunity presented itself working with ex-bankers he knew and trusted and which generated much excitement. Suddenly he had light in his eyes and the bounce back in his step, yet he hesitated. We went through the numbers, discussed

---

the more modest salary against his outgoings and I asked what was holding him back. "Having to tell my teenage daughters to turn right on an aircraft," he said. For him it was a very real consideration even when the alternative was flogging away at a job he was beginning to detest. I'm glad to be able to tell you that he chose the entrepreneurial job and didn't look back.

Lack of curiosity

Many people don't seek feedback and as a result they lack self-awareness. It is important that you seek feedback and have mentors. Effective feedback works with a strengths-based approach. Failure to learn from experience – doing the same thing over and over and getting the same result – won't help you to succeed. The same approach won't necessarily work in different environments.

Not listening

Not many people are good at spontaneously giving feedback, so when you do get some, listen and carefully consider the answer. Let's imagine you have asked a colleague for some feedback on a big client presentation you've just delivered. You may be thinking that it went rather well and be rather flushed with success. So when you hear your colleague say, "Yes I think it went well overall - especially the summary," you could ask, "What was it particularly in the summary section that you liked? What could I improve on in the earlier sections?" You might receive a lot more information to work with.

Likewise, review the interview notes and think about the "third chair" from which you can see yourself as others see you. What would the objective observer say about your performance? Are there any little nuggets of information you could use to make you stand out from the other candidates?

Failure to take risks

Be brave, be bold. The only thing holding you back is you. Susan Jeffers PhD, author of the best-selling book entitled "Feel the fear and do it anyway", has helped many people overcome their fears and move forward in life. Amusingly, she tells the story of the difficulty she faced when first trying to get this book accepted by a publisher. She says the worst rejection letter she received said: "Lady Di could be bicycling nude down the street giving this book away and nobody would read it."

The valuable lesson she learned at that point was never give up if you believe in something!

Objective assessment

Many applications head for the bin because applicants have neglected to look objectively at themselves in relation to the job that they hope to get. This is an essential part of your strategy if you want to avoid:

· Wasting time and effort applying for work which is not really right for you.
· Forgetting to mention those qualities which make you the right person for the job.
· Failing to recognise that, although you might be the right person in the long term, in the short term you lack important skills and experience.

Many speculative applications fail to hit their target because the writer hasn't been clear about the sort of job for which they are applying.

Failure to actively seek feedback

If you are unsuccessful, it is a good idea to get feedback from the interviewer because

- this shows you are still keen on the job and demonstrates a professional attitude There may be a time when you are needed. For example, if the first choice person cannot take the position or another suitable vacancy arises;
- the feedback will help with your job hunt. It pays to treat each interview as a learning opportunity.

If you do ask for feedback, make sure that you take it well. Do not argue - you may not always like to hear negative feedback but the purpose of the call is to help you in the future. You asked for an opinion – respect it and use it positively.

I'd like to end this chapter with a story that I heard from a former colleague, Cathy Hackett. She was trying to convince an organisation I worked for that we needed to make significant changes. She showed us a video from her holiday in New Zealand; it was of her doing a bungee jump. We saw her walk to edge, saw the abyss. She said it was the scariest thing she'd ever done but somehow she found courage and jumped over. It was, she said, the most exhilarating thing she'd ever done. That's what change is like - when you stand on the edge it's scary but you have to make that leap. To achieve something worthwhile you may find that you have to start from a really scary place. As the diplomat, James Bryant Conant said: *"Behold the turtle: he only makes progress when he sticks his neck out."*

Part 2

Short term: Tactical actions you need to take

University of
South Wales
Prifysgol
De Cymru

Library Services

Chapter 7

The Proactive Job Search

"Go confidently in the direction of your dreams! Live the life you've imagined."

Henry David Thoreau

What this chapter tells you about Everlasting Employability:

- Target organisations that have the propensity to hire people with your skill set.
- Identify the point of purchase (the person with the power to hire you).
- Use your network to set up a meeting with the point of purchase.

The majority of jobs are never advertised. So just sending out your CV to agencies or headhunters simply isn't going to get a worthwhile result. It's a waste of time. Your CV has to be aimed at carefully chosen targets.

If you need to reinvent your career then you need to understand your job market.

If you have been working your way through this book, then you will have already considered your career options, know what job you want and what skills and competencies you need to get it. You have to produce a development plan for the skills, knowledge and expertise you need to be the best possible candidate.

How do you persuade an employer to hire you so that you can gain the skills you do not have? Recruiters tend to want to hire only those with the prerequisite skills, so you are debarred from selection if you want but do not have this skill set. In reality there has to be a good business reason for an employer to hire you, so the skill gap has to be reasonably small.

Hiring good people is exceptionally difficult even in the present climate. If you are able to demonstrate how you can add value to a prospective employer, increase revenues, decrease cost, then you will always get a hearing. The trick is getting in front of the employer to demonstrate that potential added value. So where do you start?

Identify who has the power to hire you — the "point of purchase". The wider your network, the greater your chances of success. But recognise that an introduction will only get you the meeting, not the job. Don't worry at this point if you are immediately thinking that your network is small or non- existent. There's a whole chapter devoted to the power of networking, and in practice we find that people have much better networks than they first think.

The proactive job search requires you to be prepared, proactive, systematic and organised. There is a form to help you achieve this in the appendices.

Finding out where the jobs are and how to find them is just one aspect of looking for a job. You need to understand how to apply this knowledge to your job-hunting so that you can use the information effectively. The proactive job search methodology is about finding someone in your network who can recommend you to the point of purchase. Fundamentally it's a different way of job seeking. You, the candidate, find the organisation in which you want to work by proactively making contact through recommendation.

The spreadsheet for the proactive job searcher is in the Appendix. You probably need to build something similar in Excel, as it should grow like Topsy. You need to do the following:

1. Identify the organisations likely to hire people with your skill set.
2. Consider the characteristics of the sort of company you would like to work for and where you would do well.
3. Identify the point of purchase – the decision-maker – not the HR department, they are the gatekeepers.
4. Find out what can you about them – network, use your sources, LinkedIn, reference materials.

Compared to the traditional route of replying to adverts and cold calling, this is a more dynamic and efficient method of looking for the job that suits you rather than just a vacancy that needs to be filled.

Here are some activities that could help you find those hidden jobs:

- List your friends/contacts (and their jobs) and ask them for advice.
- Build your network with as many people as possible looking for you and let contacts know you're around and available.
- Keep in touch with changes in your field – scan the journals, trade magazines, newsletters and the web.
- Go to continuous professional development (CPD) events - you'll find some listed on LinkedIn and other specialist websites in your field.
- Go to local business events and use the reference library as you will gain access to a wide range of journals and information without paying subscriptions. Keep an eye out for relevant snippets of useful information to send to your network as a way of staying in touch.
- Build new networks by attending local/regional meetings of professional associations, bodies or groups or get involved in community projects or voluntary activities.
- Volunteer to work unpaid or on a trial basis (especially in small firms). Use any opportunity to show your ability and make new contacts.

Persistence is the key to successfully achieving your goals. Don't become distracted making excuses about why things can't be done. Remember Bob the Builder – "Can you do it?" Yes, you can.

Target potential employers and network to get introductions, to set up exploratory meetings and to get an interview date. To do this well you need to build up your network, so you'll need to look at the following chapters covering networking and social media.

You should aim to have a big and effective enough network that you can reach 40-70% of your target organisations fairly readily via networking.

Your network includes clients, colleagues and professional peers, suppliers, and your friends and family.

Your target organisations are likely to comprise competitors to your current employer. Moving within an industry that already uses and recognises your skills, qualifications and experience is the easiest route to new employment.

However you may need to expand your options if the job market is tight or if you want the challenge of a change of sector. So think about your clients and suppliers as potential targets. You'll use the same skills but in a different arena and different culture. The leap from working in HR at a bank to being an HR practitioner in a pharmaceutical manufacturer is not so very great, although if there are other candidates for the role with same sector experience you may find the competition stiff!

Consider what else you want from the move. If finding a job with a much shorter commute is important, your target list needs to be focused on your immediate locality and your networking needs to address this.

Think about what will impress potential employers. If you take the time and trouble to get someone to make a recommendation on your behalf, that's going to play in your favour. A recommendation won't necessarily result in an interview or a job offer but it will expand your network. If you network well you should get to hear about potential roles. If the vacancies are there and you don't get invited for interview then review your CV and the effectiveness of your networking.

If your network endorses your reputation and is recommending you and networking on your behalf, you should at least be shortlisted. An employer is going to look twice at the candidate recommended by someone he or she knows. That has to be a better bet than sending a mail-shot out blindly to hundreds of companies or better even than the CV sent in by a head-hunter alongside several others, especially if you are an unknown candidate.

Chapter 8

Networking

"The successful networkers I know, the ones receiving tons of referrals and feeling truly happy about themselves, continually put the other person's needs ahead of their own."

Bob Burg

What this chapter tells you about Everlasting Employability:

- The proactive job search requires a networking introduction.
- Why most people misunderstand what networking is and therefore don't like doing it.
- The Good Samaritan principle that underpins all networking activity is adding value to others.
- Creating a networking CRM (client relationship management) system.
- 3 killer questions that every job-seeking networker needs to ask.
- Adding value and how to get advice.
- Networking logistics.
- Making effective use of your network.
- The importance of elevator pitches.
- An idiot's guide to good interpersonal skills.

The proactive job search is about identifying and targeting where you might be hired. It's also about using your network to make contact with those people defined as "point of purchase" so as to get interviews.

Your network is made up of four main categories of people – colleagues, clients, suppliers and professional peers. However, as you never know where a network connection may arise, you should always include your friends and extended family.

When you are job seeking you need a minimum of 250 people in your network. You should be aiming for an overall network of 350 people who are constantly feeding information through to you and to whom you respond with information that is useful to them. This may sound a lot but with the advent of social media networks it has been made much easier. Even 50 people may sound a lot when you are first starting to network but you'll soon get the hang of it.

Your network is made up of all sorts of people. Segment your network on two levels: Firstly the strength of your relationship and secondly their sphere of influence.

The ones who can help most with the job search are those with whom you have a strong relationship and whose level of influence is high. When you are trying to target companies and points of purchase within those organisations, use your network to make those links. You need to get in front of the right person. Network to get there.

My premise is that actually most people don't understand networking. What I call the Good Samaritan principle applies to networking. It's about adding value, helping people in your network with no expectation of anything in return. The significance in terms of employability is that you need the network in order to source opportunities. It's a bit like a bank account. You add to it by helping other people. So when you need help it's a good idea to be in credit before you need to start drawing down the favours.

Most people do it the other way round, they start networking when they need help and so start from an overdraft position.

In broad terms people like to help, if they can, if it's not too much trouble and if you ask nicely. And if they know you'll be willing to help them before they even ask, you're in credit on the brownie points.

A lot of people say they are bad at networking and claim to hate it. What they fear, what they don't like to have to do, is contacting people they haven't seen for years. They think the other party will "suss" them and think they are being used. If you only contact people when you need something from them, you will feel like a user, most people would. So ask them for their advice, ask them how they got into this career, ask them what the challenges are, ask them questions as though you are a consultant or researcher not a job seeker. Start with warm contacts to build your confidence. Always consider what might be helpful information for the other person, something you can offer them.

As your confidence grows you will find that if you had a good relationship with people several years ago, they will still be pleased to hear from you even now. However, think carefully about your approach. You could for example comment on their profile on LinkedIn and send them a leading article that might be of interest to them along the lines of "I saw this and thought of you."

© 2012 Ted Goff

"You have now been
networked. Next!"

The other big mistake is that so many people seem to think that networking is about going to networking events such as the dreaded conference. What they hate about the conference or event is the problem of how to break into small groups of people who are already talking to each other. Nobody wants to be left out. It's the same at a dinner party, the fear that the people on either side of you will start talking to others and you'll be left out. Nobody wants to be a wallflower.

To get the best out of a networking event, don't go late hoping that the party will have warmed up a bit by the time you get there, and don't go with a friend if you are going to stick to them like glue all evening. The whole point is to make new contacts and expand your knowledge. So take a deep breath and go early! You'll find that the organisers will be delighted to greet you. Ask them who they are expecting to come and scan the list for anyone you might like to meet. If you spot the name of someone you'd like to meet, ask the organisers if they wouldn't mind introducing you to this person when they arrive. After that, when people start to arrive, act like a host. Stand near the entrance, welcome new people, invite them to join your group and introduce them to each other. This on its own will make people feel grateful! Nobody likes turning up and being alone in a group of strangers. It may also be your means of exiting one group. For example you may say "Hello, would you like to join us? Did you say your name was Nicola? Let me introduce Fred here. He was just telling me a fascinating story about how he....." and leave!

You can always join new groups by asking just that: "Do you mind if I join you?" I've never been told "No!" yet. However some groups are easier to join than others. People who are standing openly in a small semi-circle are open to people joining. People standing face to face probably know each other well, have a lot to catch up on and won't welcome the interruption. Always have a business card to exchange when needed, make a quick note on theirs regarding a mutual point of interest for follow up and when and where you met them, as it's amazing how quickly you can forget! The following day you can send them a quick polite email or add them to your network on LinkedIn.

Networking effectively is hard work with no certainty of reward. In fact, you have to kiss a lot of frogs before you find a prince. I did tell you at the outset that this was not for the fainthearted. There is no easy way of making sure that you are employable. You have to work at it.

So what makes a good networker?
Good networkers are easily accessible. They are friendly. They smile and are welcoming, however or whenever, you meet them. When you talk to them, they are responsive. They are quick to return calls and emails.

Also important is that good networkers are usually knowledgeable. They offer advice and expertise, the sort of information that is usually something you have not already thought of. They give you leads and they introduce you to their contacts.

If you think about it, you are probably comfortable networking at a personal level - asking a neighbour for a recommendation for a local dentist for example. You may not realise it, but asking for information and resources to get a job done at work is also a form of networking. It is usually only the third, strategic, category in which people need help in re-framing their ideas about networking.

If you can network in the first or second of these categories, consider what you can learn and use to be a strategic networker.

Good networkers take pleasure in being a conduit. Almost like a marriage broker they like bringing people together. They like to see others benefit from what they have done.

Good networkers trade information, so there is a by-product resulting from the proactive job search. Even though this will not be classified information you can still get a much richer vein of information from talking to a target organisation's direct employees. I suggested earlier that you focus on a specific sector or a narrow group of companies. So by the time you have met up with two or three organisations in that sector you'll have quite a bit of market intelligence. You can trade that with other target companies because most people tend to be quite myopic and don't bother too much about finding out what their competitors are up to. So you can add value.

	Personal	Operational	Strategic
Purpose	Enhancing personal and professional development; providing referrals to useful information and contacts.	Getting work done efficiently; maintaining the capacities and functions required of the group.	Figuring out future priorities and challenges; getting stakeholder support for them.
Location and temporal orientation	Contacts are mostly external and oriented toward current interests and future potential interests.	Contacts are mostly internal and oriented toward current demands.	Contacts are internal and external and oriented toward the future.
Players and recruitment	Key contacts are mostly discretionary; it is not always clear who is relevant.	Key contacts are relatively nondiscretionary; they are prescribed mostly by the task and organisational structure, so it is very clear who is relevant.	Key contacts follow from the strategic context and the organisational environment, but specific membership is discretionary; it is not always clear who is relevant.
Network attributes and key behaviours	Breadth: reaching out to contacts who can make referrals.	Depth: building strong working relationships.	Leverage: creating inside-outside links.

Adapted from the Harvard Business Review

Love it or hate it networking is a sure way of increasing your access to new employment opportunities. Dale Carnegie, 71 years ago in his book 'How to Win Friends and Influence People', explored the importance of developing and maintaining relationships for mutual benefit at all stages of career development.

And it's not just about professional help - assist wherever you can. It could be anything from discount deals, good restaurants, reliable plumbers as well as trading information about jobs and potential roles.

Good networkers follow up and they don't look for rewards. So, if you don't like doing it or are shy of doing it or really bad at doing it, this is how you start.

1. The first thing is to create a database of your network. Put simply a list of everyone in your network. A spread sheet or a little black book will do.

2. List all the people you know in the four categories we already mentioned – colleagues, clients, suppliers, professional peers. This is really great because what you are doing is creating your Christmas card list nice and early.

3. Start it right now before you need it. And if you need it you must start straight away.

4. Create time to network inside your organisation and outside. Give it at least two hours a week, one networking meeting inside and one outside and typically do that at lunch or over coffee. When you are meeting people you are collecting data which in the first instance you use to populate your database.

5. Make sure you capture what people tell you on your spread sheet. Make notes about them, what they said, who they know – this will enable you to see how they can help you and crucially how you can help them.

Does that sound manipulative? Well if you have a good memory and can remember 300 or so people, that's great, but most people can't. So you have to have a system that you can use diligently and intelligently.

I once met someone from private banking who told me that when he met a client for the first time he paid particular attention to whether they chose tea or coffee and whether they took sugar. So the next time he met them he could say "do you still take one sugar?" It worked a treat because people were touched that he took a personal interest and remembered. So make notes - what is the name of your contact's spouse, how many children, what hobbies?

Networking for the job seeker

In the context of the proactive job search, networking is key. But before you go out there asking advice from your network, one of the first things to do is to look for a trusted adviser.

Consider your network of people, those you know extremely well who are also influential, the sort of people you might see as a mentor.

Arrange to meet and ask three questions.
1. Having shared your elevator pitch – check what they have heard. Did the message land?
2. Can I do it? Ask someone you really trust and ask them to be honest. There is no point going after a job if someone you trust doesn't think you can do that job, that's just a waste of time and energy.
3. How did you come across? Was I too nervous, too "in your face"? How did I appear? Anxious, over-confident?

Finding a job is going to take around three months, maybe more, but if you have planned your career you should be thinking about your next move a year or more before you start the job search. You should be using your network and building your contacts with that goal in mind.

Now what I want to do is give you the basic structure of a networking conversation for job seeking. I am assuming at this point that you have, as recommended, done your background research on the person you are meeting and the organisation they work for!

The first golden rule is this: This is not about you. It is about them. What do I mean by that? Spend the first part of the meeting focussing on them. How you do this will depend on how well you know them. Either you are re-establishing the link with them or forging a new link. So if it is someone you once worked with, reminisce about old times; or if it is someone who has been recently introduced then talk about them.

The real skill is to listen to what they tell you. By talking about them, both in personal and professional terms, you should hear things which you can use to add value. So in a business setting, for example, you might be talking about the challenges facing a business, you might ask how they arose or what the opportunities are and what they need to do to exploit those opportunities.

If you are talking personal stuff, can you recommend restaurants they might visit if they are going on holiday somewhere you have been? Or a good decorator? Look for something where you can add value. If you can help or have useful information, then say so, volunteer it. Be generous with your knowledge as it will pay you dividends in the long run.

The main thing to remember is that you are going to ask advice at some point, NOT for a job, but for advice. This advice might be that you need an introduction to a company or suggestions of companies that might need your skill set. Before you ask, say something nice but be sincere. If you say something thoughtful and complimentary about a person they are more than likely to help you. If it is someone you know, you might tell them that they are someone you respect or that they seem to have good knowledge of the market. If it is someone you don't know and met through a third party, tell them how highly the third party regards them.

Then pop the question you have in mind. Do NOT ask for a job. Ask for advice.

When you leave the meeting, follow up. This is the biggest mistake that most people make, they fail to follow up. If you have been given a lead or told that help will be forthcoming, make sure that you contact the lead or that the help comes through.

If you don't contact a lead you have been given you have wasted your time. You have also wasted the valuable time and knowledge of your contact and possibly their goodwill. So it is really important that you have the discipline to capture and record what you have been told so you can do something useful with it.

If you find that your contact doesn't do what they said they would, don't despair. It doesn't mean that they won't do it or they lack the will. It is not because they don't want to help, it's just that life gets in way. So the smart thing to do is to try to make it easy for them. Ask – "if you haven't had time to contact them, can I call them and use your name?"

It is important to keep your active contacts in your line of sight. In other words, keep them current. One meeting does not constitute a relationship. Relationships come from seeing people at least three times over a 12-18 month period. So keep in touch.

You need to keep people in sight so that you can continue to add value. Perhaps you might spot something in the press that might interest your contact which you can pass on to them. It could be that someone tells you of an opportunity that might be of interest to your contact. Or it might be something more personal that will catch their attention.

This is another reason to collect data on the people in your network, so you can think of ways to keep dialogue open. Send a note asking how the holiday was? Ask if they enjoyed it? But don't be a stalker! By keeping in touch and helping them, they will help you.

Just a few words on networking and logistics. Particularly when you are job seeking the significance of getting round your network will not have escaped you. But networking is bad for the waistline - drinking coffee and eating out take their toll. You can only have one lunch a day. So smart networkers regretfully turn down invitations for lunch while suggesting "Can we meet up for half an hour?" Go for a coffee, or even better if you've had at least one coffee already, a black tea, or drop in to meet in their office. A great advantage to being on their territory is that you can collect the data and it's easier to record. Take a notebook with you to record the information you uncover. If it doesn't seem right there and then, do it straight afterwards, making notes particularly about any market intelligence you pick up. Bars or busy restaurants are difficult places to make notes in.

For any job seeker, networking properly is hard work. It seems so much easier to give your CV to some recruiter and let them do all the work. When you were junior that was fine as it was the usual way to move jobs. At more senior levels you have to be much more proactive. Opportunities won't drop into your lap, you have to seek them out.

In the public sector where rules and regulations relating to recruitment are so stringent, you may be wondering if this still applies. So if you are doubtful whether networking will work for you, here's a question: Do you think it helps that someone on the appointments panel knows you?

Of course it does. They are much more likely to shortlist you because they know you or know of you. If you've been recommended by someone who already works for them or by someone who they trust, you have a tailor-made advantage over the other candidates.

The alternative is to sit and wait. Do you think that will work? Do you really think the perfect job is going to pop out of the woodwork?

Is it worth being part of a professional body? What do you think? Will it help to build your network by interfacing with like-minded individuals? Of course it will. Go to local networking events and build your contact database.

Do you think a mentor adds value to your network? Do you think you should share your career aspirations? Be realistic. Use your network to get advice on developing your aspirational competencies. We explored the value of a mentor in chapter 5.

The key is always to share but don't be a bore. Don't spend too long in transmit mode. Many people are one-way networkers. Don't be a user, who only makes contact when you need something from someone. The key to good networking is reciprocity.

Networking is the key to your job search. The foundations of the network you develop with your on-going relationship-building meetings and all that reciprocity are what you will use to build the long-term career plan.

You've heard it many times: "It's not what you know but who you know". Networking activities will significantly build and enhance your sphere of influence.

Advice for the active and empowered jobseeker:

- Maintain a positive outlook. Even if you've been made redundant, don't play the victim — learn to see change as an opportunity.
- Make sure you use the resources of your network, get a mentor to help you focus and formulate your plans.
- Think about your career plan moving forward.
- Target employers and network to get yourself in front of them.

The idea of networking is to approach people you know or who are known to people you know, for help and advice. Every time you make a new contact you then tap into their network and get introductions to a new range of contacts. You gradually build up a large list of people who can help you.

If you're not sure about networking, bear in mind:

- You've probably already used networking skills more than you realised. For example, you've probably asked a neighbour for advice or information on a babysitter, school or dentist without thinking twice about it and without considering it to be a form of networking.
- There are many established networks that you can use such as university alumni.
- Most people are flattered to be approached for advice - it is indicative that you respect their opinion and they will therefore be happy to talk to you.
- Other people do it - we know that most vacancies are filled through networks - so if you don't you'll lose out to those who do!
- Many people establish successful careers through networking. Think of how politicians lobby for support. Lobbying is just a more assertive form of networking!
- You can ask politely for help and people can always say no
- You'll still need to prove you have what it takes to do the job, so it is just a way of identifying opportunities

Build up your contacts
Warm leads are easier to use than cold ones so it's always best to start with people with whom you have an acquaintance in common. As you get more confident at networking you will find yourself asking for help from people who you hardly know at all. As an illustration, I can think of an occasion once when a colleague and I were waiting in freezing conditions for a taxi to the station after a client meeting. After an interminable wait,

one taxi arrived which we gratefully climbed into leaving a stranger on the pavement. We held the door open to him and asked if we could drop him off en route to the station. He was pleased to do so and during the course of the journey he asked us some questions about what we did for a living. We swapped cards and a week or so later he approached us again and commissioned a piece of work. You never know where your conversations might lead!

Even if you can't think of people who could help you directly, someone from within your network is likely to know somebody who could give you some advice. One of your contacts may belong to a well established network, such as a professional association, a livery company, an alumni group and have contacts of their own who can help you.

List your current colleagues and think about which of them you would be happy to approach for advice. Consider ex-colleagues who are in new organisations or external suppliers you have come into contact with and add them to your list.

Be proactive and seek out opportunities in the marketplace. Ask people about their work challenges and see if you can spot any shortfalls - you may be able to tell them about a similar scenario and what you did in those circumstances. This may be free advice that they will value and whilst we do say don't ask directly for a job, there may be occasions when you may feel that the time is right to ask more subtly "do you need any help with that?"

Ask your contacts for recruitment contacts as a lead-in will always be better than calling cold.

And promise yourself you won't let your contacts go dormant until the next time you need a new job.

There are lots of people with no connection to you at all who may be able to offer you advice. Those most likely to help are people whose job role involves providing help and advice. Whilst e-mail is fine for making contact, try to find people you'll be able to telephone or speak to face-to-face for advice as not many people have time to write lengthy replies to letters or e-mails.

Professional bodies often employ information officers and training advisers who can talk to you over the phone. They may publish a directory of members. They may have a local branch that you can join or a network of regional advisers.

Courses and events are a good way of meeting those who could give you advice, e.g. specialist recruitment fairs for specific industries, trade fairs, conferences and short courses.

If you are seeking an internal role then you need to network across the breadth of your organisation. This will be invaluable as you will glean far more information than if you are an outsider. It's always possible that you will find problem areas that have not yet been condensed into a job specification.

Redundancy does not necessarily close off internal opportunities but most organisations pay lip service to the idea of redeployment, so be proactive. Your HR department will only have roles that are signed off and if you don't fit the role perfectly you are unlikely to be considered. Perhaps you will be able to create a role for yourself if you have good advocates within the firm. After all, the organisation that knows you best is your current employer. They are most likely to offer you an opportunity to develop your aspirational competencies as they already know your capabilities. Network internally; share your view of the future with your current employer to see if you can make an internal career transition.

Network, network, network. People who are really successful are well connected, both inside and outside the organisation. The people skills you develop through networking are essential as you move into more senior positions. They will also give you a competitive advantage over the course of your career.

Be ready to spot and respond to opportunities. Seek assignments outside your area of expertise or normal job responsibilities. Initiative and well-rounded skills will impress your managers and increase your visibility within the company, making you someone for management to watch and develop.

Do some external networking so you know what is cutting edge for other organisations. As you rise through an organisation it will help if you appreciate the bigger picture and can distinguish between what's really important and what will have no real impact on the bottom line.

Making effective use of contacts

Plan the objectives for your networking before you start contacting people for advice, and decide what you want to get out of your networking campaign.

Research each contact, their role and their organisation, before making an approach and keep impeccable records. Try to get a personal introduction if you possibly can.

You will impress a contact more at a first meeting if you have some recent and relevant knowledge. If you have found out about a contact through someone you know, then you should be able to get some background information. You'll be able to do some initial research on them and their company.

Make a list of questions for each discussion, so if you are asking for career advice:

- What are the major tasks/responsibilities of your job?
- How did you get into this job?
- What are the skills/attributes required?
- What are the positive/negative aspects or challenges/problems of your job?
- How are vacancies in the industry or at that company advertised?
- Could you tell me about related jobs in a similar field? This is to broaden your outlook
- Could you refer me to someone else to talk to in the industry? May I use your name?

Some points to consider:

- Some kinds of approach may be acceptable to one contact but not to another. Most will probably prefer a phone call rather than having to reply to a letter or e-mail.
- The better you know someone, the more informal your approach to them can be.
- Good communication skills are needed for direct approaches.
- Your call should elicit some kind of immediate feedback.
- Before you call, note what you plan to say and keep this by you.
- Combine a written approach with a direct approach. You could email your contact a copy of your CV, but only if you think it won't put them under pressure and/or if you are certain that there is something in it that will interest them. If you are not sure then don't include it. Then arrange to call them at a specific time.

Always note any action points. And then follow up on all of them.

Thank your contact for their help, even if you can't really use the information or they weren't very helpful. Thank them anyway.

Networking with charm

Nobody wants to be bothered by nuisance calls or junk mail, so don't come across like an unwanted salesperson! Needy is not attractive to most of us, especially if we are a hiring manager. You must:

- Start with contacts with whom you have a fairly direct link - they're more likely to want to help.
- Explain how you got their details and outline the help you need.
- Start by asking for their opinion.
- Don't be too pushy. Don't get aggressive. Don't be too smart.
- Thank them and follow up with a written thank you too.

Effective networking requires effort, organisation and a certain amount of courage, but

- it will improve your career direction and prospects,
- it will be useful to you in other aspects of your life, and
- you'll develop your interpersonal skills and your self-confidence.

Elevator pitch

The elevator pitch is so called because in the time it takes for a lift to ascend or descend a building you are able to deliver your marketing proposition. This is your opportunity to tell your network what it is you are looking for. An elevator pitch is made up of three components:

1. Where you have come from, your career to date.
2. Why you left or are planning to leave your current employer.
3. What your short and long term goals are.

Elevator pitches are best delivered as a story of the journey of your career. The reason for leaving is always delivered in a positive manner but should be the filling in the sandwich, with more time spent on where you have come from and where you want to go. Never slag-off previous employers or bosses. Always highlight the positives of your current employment situation. However, the majority of time should be spent on your destination. Smart candidates know their ultimate destination and how the next job features in reaching that destination. This message must be delivered with enthusiasm. It gives you the opportunity to make your network aware of potential employers for whom you would like to work, as well as the opportunity to source other networking introductions to help you reach your destination.

I strongly advise you to road test your elevator pitch prior to commencing a job search campaign. You should write out your script and learn your lines. An elevator pitch should take no more than 5 minutes to deliver. We only remember about a third of what we hear and indeed most of what we take in is visual. We will refer to the psychology of receiving information later in the chapter on interviewing, however the reason for learning your lines is so you can concentrate on delivery and, more importantly, how the message is being received.

In preparing your marketing campaign I recommend you test the elevator pitch on two trusted advisors. These are the people with whom you have a strong personal relationship and they have what I call power of influence. That means if they make a call on your behalf someone will take it. Typically these are the people you regard as mentors.

You need to deliver your elevator pitch and then ask them three questions.

1. What did you hear? This will test if the message landed correctly.
2. Can I achieve this goal? It is essential they give you their endorsement. That is why you need someone who knows you well and will be honest in their feedback. There is no point embarking on this job search if they feel you can't achieve your goal.

3. Check how you came over when delivering this message. Were you too pushy or too laid-back for example?

The elevator pitch is a very, very important part of your employability strategy. The more people who know of it, as the eyes and ears of your network, the greater the likelihood of career success. You should always have an elevator pitch even when you are not actively job searching. It's the story of your career journey. It should be interesting and memorable. It must always be delivered with passion.

Developing good interpersonal skills
A slight digression here. William of Wykeham said in the 14th century that "manners maketh man" and it is still true. Etiquette does still matter and it's important for networking and for your future career.

Think about how you are perceived by your manager and colleagues. It's important for your personal happiness at the office and for the future of your career.

No matter how hard you work or how many brilliant ideas you may have, if you don't connect with people around you your professional life will suffer.

So here are some tips on building good interpersonal skills.

Smile. Most people don't like to be around those who grouch, not for long anyway. Do your best to be friendly and upbeat with your co-workers. Maintain a positive, cheerful attitude about work and about life. Smile often. The positive energy you radiate will draw others to you. If your nickname is 'Rottweiler' you may be doing something wrong!

Appreciate stuff. Find something positive about everyone you work with and let them hear it. Be generous with praise and kind words of encouragement. Say thank you when someone helps you. Make colleagues feel welcome when they call or stop by your office. If you let others know that they are appreciated, they'll want to give you their best.

Pay attention. Observe what's going on with other people. Acknowledge their happy milestones, express concern or sympathy in difficult situations such as an illness or bereavement. Make eye contact and call people by their first names. Ask for their opinions. Praise good work and good ideas.

Active listening. If you listen actively it shows that you hear and understand another's point of view. You can do this by good eye contact and body language. You might nod to show you've understood a point or summarise briefly what they've said. It shows that you understood their meaning and they know that your responses are more than lip service. Your colleagues will appreciate knowing you are really listening to what they say.

Bring together. Create an environment that encourages team work. Treat everyone equally, don't play favorites. Don't talk about others behind their backs. Follow up people's suggestions or requests. If you make a statement or announcement, check to see that you have been understood. If people see you as someone reliable and fair, they will trust you.

Resolve conflict. Go beyond simply bringing people together, become someone who resolves conflicts as they arise. Learn to be an effective mediator. If colleagues bicker, arrange to sit down and help sort out differences.

Communicate clearly. Pay attention to what you say and how you say it. A clear and effective communicator avoids misunderstandings with colleagues and associates. Verbal eloquence projects an image of intelligence and maturity, no matter what your age. If you tend to blurt out anything that comes to mind, people won't give much weight to your words or opinions.

Humour. Don't be afraid to be funny or clever. Most people are drawn to a person who can make them laugh. Use your sense of humour to overcome barriers and gain people's affection.

See both sides. Empathy is the ability to put yourself in someone else's shoes and understand how they feel. It's not the same as sympathy. Try to view situations and responses from another person's perspective and withhold your own judgment and perspectives. Stay in touch with your own emotions; those who are cut off from their own feelings are often unable to empathize with others.

Do not complain. There is nothing worse than a chronic complainer or whiner. If you have to vent about something, save it for your diary or a trusted confidant who has no stake in the situation. If you must verbalise your grievances, keep it short. After all, is the person known around the office as "Whiny Fred" going to be top of the list when recommendations are sought for an interesting opportunity?

Chapter 9

Using LinkedIn and other social media sites

"You jump off a cliff and you assemble an aeroplane on the way down."
Reid Hoffman, founder of LinkedIn explaining the complexities of starting a business.

What this chapter tells you about Everlasting Employability:

- How LinkedIn and the other social media tools will help you develop a network.
- How to create your profile.
- The importance of an on-line profile and in particular the power of recommendations.
- How to search companies for someone who knows you.
- Using Groups and other social media tools to increase visibility and add value to your network.

When I first devised the proactive job search methodology I used to refer to "linking" someone who knows you to the point of purchase. Little did I know that LinkedIn would appear and apply technology to that process.

LInkedIn is the reluctant networker's friend. It helps identify the point of purchase, tells you all about them, and it shows you how you are connected to them. It also allows you, via email, to re-establish contacts with those you haven't spoken to in years without an awkward and possibly embarrassing conversation.

It is revolutionising the search industry as headhunters can use it to identify and reference candidates. It has spawned the growth of in-house search teams, as organisations find they can significantly reduce their recruitment costs and build their own database of prospective candidates.

You need to appreciate that any networking meeting or interview will result in you being checked out either before or after.

© 2009 Ted Goff

"Somewhere in here is us, and somewhere else is our big success. We need to find the path that connects the two."

It is for this reason, if none other, that you should be a member of LinkedIn and give very careful thought as to how you present yourself on the web.

I am now going to introduce you to someone who is, in my opinion, the UK's No.1 authority on LinkedIn. Lincoln Coutts, one of those really clever social media/techie sorts of guys to whom every job seeker needs access. He has written the greater part of this chapter for which I am indebted to him.

What is LinkedIn?

There are numerous websites out there aimed at helping you network and share information, the main one, for business purposes, is LinkedIn.

LinkedIn, as a site, was founded at the end of 2002 and launched in May 2003. For most people it's a site usually introduced to them by a colleague.

One of the original ideas for the site was to allow users to create and develop their network as they moved through their career. The site allows you to invite contacts to become a direct connection and, using a principal loosely based on six degrees of separation, it will allow you to view people in the first three degrees of your network who you know through common connections.

In June 2012 membership of LinkedIn reached 175 million.

Getting started: What to include and what to omit

I am on record as saying that people spend too much time on their CV. I do not share the conventional thinking that the CV is at the very heart of a job search. I place much more importance on networking an introduction to a point of purchase, whereas the CV is a leave-behind, something that will remind your network contact or recruiter of you. However, I readily accept that your on-line presence is very important. I believe it to be replacing the CV. The on-line presence is dynamic; it gives you the opportunity to showcase your skills. It allows you to advertise yourself, publish testimonials and demonstrate your knowledge on specialist subjects of your choice. So whilst I see the CV of declining importance in your search for everlasting employability, your LinkedIn profile is crucial to that objective.

The starting point when using LinkedIn is to construct a profile based on your CV. The temptation is to cut and paste information across from your CV. Under NO circumstances do that. The reason for this is that your profile is keyword searchable so only go into the detail around the areas in which you want to work. If you were once an insurance salesman but never want to work in the field again, only mention the role and company rather than go into detail.

Your LinkedIn profile allows you to set out your stall. It is in effect the web version of your elevator pitch. Use all the sections available to you. Starting at the top, create a headline (this isn't a job title but more about what you do). Secondly, choose an industry that relates either to the one you want to work in or to the type of role you perform.

For location choose the postcode for where you want to work (not where you live, if they are different).

Your next aim is to create a summary. This is similar to your elevator pitch. Talk about who you are and what you are proud of. You can even discuss what you are looking for here. Then add some specialties. These again should be focused on you and what you have done. This section can include a heading and then a brief sentence to help set the context.

When it comes to experience, this is where you discuss current and past roles. Don't just add job titles and a company name. Some titles mean different things in different industries. You should go into detail about the jobs you've done that match your future aims, or the ones which help to prove relevant experience. This is no time to be bashful - advertise your achievements. Focus on business benefits.

Under education, don't just list your school, college or university qualifications; add some information on the subject or titles of papers you've written.

For "interests", don't just add the usual "I support Southampton FC" or "read books".   Boring! Boring! Give the viewer an insight into your personality, talk about more than just bland facts. Corporate social responsibility is very much flavour of the moment, so make reference to volunteering. There is clearly an opportunity to link your business acumen to good causes.

Photograph

It is essential you publish a photo. If for no other reason it will help those meeting you for the first time to identify you. It should be recent and taken in a professional business setting. I once met a journalist who was using a photo of her holding a gun against someone's head. Her explanation was that it was taken at a James Bond party. Whilst plausible, it does make you wonder if she had thought about her brand! Perhaps a more delicate issue is the practice of publishing photographs obviously taken some considerable time ago. I think you know what I mean. You are fooling no one. If your appearance is giving you cause for concern, visit an image consultant and or get the photograph taken professionally.

Building your network on LinkedIn

Once you've built a good profile the next step is to build your network. In my opinion you need a minimum of 500 people in your network. LinkedIn will very helpfully suggest people you may know based on what you tell it about previous employers and educational background. It does this more each and every time you visit the site. So allocating at least one hour per week to play on LinkedIn will quickly pay dividends as you build your network.

The site allows you to upload your contacts from an email account, and then matches the email address you have on file with LinkedIn users and shows if they are already using the site. This is a quick way to grow your network. But a word of caution here: it is very easy to accidentally send an invitation to everyone. Make sure you don't.

The second option for growing your network relates to your profile. The site will match other users who have also stated that they worked for a company at the same time as you; this is a great way to find former colleagues. A similar method also applies to the education information entered by users.

Whenever you see someone you want to connect with make sure you send a personal note; doing so is a great way to remind them of who you are, and helps you set out the context for your invitation. Given that you are sending an invitation, which you hope they will accept, the least you can do is say "Hi, can we catch up?" or "Great to find you on here, can we connect?" A personalised message additionally gives you the opportunity to add value to the recipient. This is the very art of networking.

There's another option available: "People you may know". This is made up of people who are connected to you by common connections, people you may have worked with and also people whose email address you have imported.

You can review how your network is made up by viewing your Network Statistics. This gives you a good indication of how your network is spread both geographically and by industry.

The site helpfully tells you how many people have viewed your profile, and how many times your name has featured in job searches in the previous 3 days. By clicking on the "your profile had been viewed" section you can get an insight into who is looking at your profile as well as seeing cumulative statistics of those looking at you.

During the course of a job search you want these statistics to show an upward trend.

Recommendations

We have always known that having met someone for the first time it is human nature to check them out. It's how we corroborate our first impressions. Of course, traditionally we turn to our network. LinkedIn very cleverly facilitates this checking out by telling you who you know in common. LinkedIn gives you the opportunity to get those who know you to give testimonials on your behalf. Having recommendations short circuits the checking out process. It enables those interested in you to see how they can connect to those in your network who are recommending you.

So how many recommendations should you publish? It goes without saying no recommendations isn't a good thing. Avoid reciprocal recommendations as it devalues the recommendations. Yes it can be tricky to get a recommendation without giving one back, but get over it. You need two or three from each employer over the last 10 years. Ideally it should be a former boss, a peer and subordinate. Remember the most important people in your network are those with whom you hold a strong relationship and who are influential. You need these people to be advocates on your behalf. You should also consider getting recommendations from clients and suppliers. The former are of particular importance if you are in a business development role. Ideally you are looking for sponsors who have gravitas within your industry and thus by association you too will be someone worth knowing. Your recommendations should always focus on specific results you have achieved. Like your CV these should be quantifiable. It isn't sufficient to say you are a nice person. Those checking you out need to see the tangible results you have achieved.

Groups
You really only want to connect to people you know. However, you can help shape your network by joining groups based on industries, locations and topics of interest. Check out the groups to which those already in your network are members. LinkedIn has thousands of groups. You are allowed to join 50, so it is important you pick wisely. Think about your

network and perceived weaknesses. LinkedIn groups give you the opportunity to develop contacts in those areas of weakness.

Groups will give you access to discussions, other members, career discussions and jobs. Whilst joining up to 50 groups might feel like a lot, you should at the very least join the groups relevant to your future career.

If you belong to a trade body, then look to see if they have a group. If they do then join it so you see what your peers are discussing. If you are looking to move industry then see what groups there are which you might choose to join as a way to find out hot topics, issues and information about the industry.

Headhunters will also create groups relevant to the industry or function in which they operate. Participation in groups is an excellent means of increasing your visibility. Remember that by sharing an update you are automatically updating your LinkedIn network.

Job section
Companies pay to advertise jobs on LinkedIn. But it's not designed to compete with some of the more common job sites.

The search options are the same as most traditional job sites, with one difference. When you view a role you are also able to see who you know in the organisations, based on your network. Also, if the hiring manager chooses to show themselves, then the site will show you if you know people in common.
You are then able to "get introduced" via the connections you have and possibly use this to assist in your application.

The job section will also recommend roles the site feels might be of interest to you based on what you state in your profile by industry, location and title.

Inbox

The inbox works in a similar way to a normal email inbox. Any message sent to you will appear here and some will also be sent to the email address you have registered on the site. You can also receive partner messages.

There may be three types of messages in your inbox. The first are messages received from your network, from introductions via your network or Inmail messages. These messages are also copied to your email account registered with LinkedIn. The second are partner messages sent by companies advertising products, services and promoting their business (you don't receive large numbers of these) and which are only sent to your inbox and not copied to your email account. The third type of messages are invitations to connect or link.

When you receive an invitation to link, it will appear in your inbox. You have four options regarding invitations:

1. The first is to accept (if you do this then the person is notified and he or she will become a 1st degree contact).
2. The second is to reply, without accepting (this allows you to send a clarifying message back to the sender without having them join your network).
3. The third option is to ignore. By doing this the person doesn't know you have done this and you can accept later.
4. The fourth option is to report as spam if you feel the message is inappropriate. The person isn't notified you have done this, however, they can see by checking the status of the message.

You can also categorise your network, thereby allowing you to selectively email to it. The tagging facility of your contacts enables you to communicate seemingly bespoke messages to your network in a group email. For example you might like to distinguish between suppliers, former colleagues, clients, friends and key influencers. This gives you the opportunity to tailor the message sent to your network, say when updating on your job search. However, beware! It is important you un-tick the "email recipients" box when sending bulk emails as otherwise all the recipients in your network will see who you are emailing and what you are doing! This facility limits you to 50 email addresses.

Companies
The "Search Company" option allows you to review information on a company, find out if you know anyone who works for that company as well as find news and press and financial data (if the company is quoted).

You can also view useful statistics on company employees. This shows details on types of roles performed in the company, qualifications employees have and the levels of experience the staff have.

You'll also be able find out about the company's growth, based on employees who you know used to work there changing their profiles. You can also find out where staff call "home" giving you an indication of the biggest international offices. Perhaps of most interest from a job searching perspective is the profiles of their recent hires and to which competitors they are losing staff. You can quickly get an insight into the industry's dynamics just by signing up to track companies.

This will also show you who you know in your network based on the 3 degrees of separation.

News
LinkedIn Today delivers top news items, tailored for you based on what your connections and industry peers are reading and sharing.

More

In this section you will find the Answers section, designed to allow you to ask or respond to questions, which are then visible to all members of LinkedIn. A great way to gain knowledge and information on topics you are not familiar with.

The Learning Centre shows short videos by way of self-help guide.

Using LinkedIn as part of your job search

LinkedIn's greatest ability is to help you be a proactive job seeker. By allowing you to target companies, you can search for more information about the point of purchase (the person with the power to hire you). It allows you to get vital background information about their work and education, their current role and perhaps most importantly how you connect to them through your LinkedIn network. LinkedIn will tell you who you already know in that company. LinkedIn gives you the facility to connect to your network connection and ask for an introduction via email to the point of purchase. Without doubt the greatest users of LinkedIn are recruiters who pay for the facility to target job searchers. This facility is open to you.

Furthermore, if you subscribe to LinkedIn you can set up alerts around job titles in order to track the movements of people holding those jobs. You can follow companies, however, without subscription. In that way you will know who is currently getting roles in the jobs you are seeking and have a window on the world of recruitment and promotions in your target companies.

Lastly and perhaps most importantly you can make it known in your profile that you are now actively seeking a new role. The use of keywords around your skill-set helps recruiters find you. LinkedIn will identify opportunities by using your job title and keyword skill-set and alert you each and every time you enter the site.

Other social media networks

In this chapter we have focused on LinkedIn as it is a professional networking site, however it won't have escaped your notice that social networking sites are springing up all over the internet. Perhaps the most famous is currently Facebook. I say "currently" as not so long ago MySpace was flavour of the month. As Yahoo discovered with the arrival of Goggle, technology and participation moves very quickly in the world of social media. As with LinkedIn, using social media for your job search could be a book in itself. However, what is really interesting about social media is that it gives you the opportunity to establish your online presence, the ability to showcase your expertise, and is therefore key to ensuring your employability.

The significance of having a presence on other social networking sites such as Facebook is that it gives the reader the opportunity to have a holistic view of you. Teacher by day, wild party animal by night is incongruous if your brand is that of a pillar of the local community and you are looking to be hired as a headmaster. Likewise, portraying yourself at interview as a family man but without pictures of your children on Facebook seems anomalous. Remember that people seeking you out will trawl the Internet, and Google aides that search by pointing out all your appearances. Hence the need for careful management. Consistency and appropriateness of your personal brand are key.

Social media can also be a "light touch" vehicle to help build your network. Many of us are reluctant to establish contact with people we haven't seen for many years. We are fearful that they will suspect our motives for getting back in touch, particularly if it is very obvious we are job searching. Facebook can be very helpful in re-establishing contact without necessarily having to declare your hand on why you have done so. Remember - Facebook is all about your friends. I read recently a very good piece of advice on inviting or accepting invitations. Would you be happy having these people over for dinner? That's the Facebook test.

Likewise Friends Reunited is a useful vehicle to track people down. However, this is another social networking tool that appears to have been overtaken by Facebook. Finally, Twitter is becoming an increasingly important way of ensuring visibility within your network. I personally don't subscribe to the Stephen Fry approach of giving a blow-by-blow account of ordinary, everyday life. However, Twitter does give you the opportunity to tweet information and articles that will add value to your network - remember my Good Samaritan principle. Twitter enables you to keep your network up to date on what you are currently working, your achievements and future intentions. The arrival of Hootsuite and Tweetdeck give you the ability to manage LinkedIn and Twitter simultaneously, by allowing simultaneous updates and tweets. However, I urge caution as this is a hand that can be overplayed. Too much self-publicity across the internet and you can lose your audience. Never use Twitter to stalk individuals. That said, social media is very much here to stay. It is a very important part of your job search and an essential part of ensuring everlasting employability. It is a great marketing tool for you.

Chapter 10

Interview preparation and positive psychology

"If you don't see yourself as a winner, then you cannot perform as a winner."

  Zig Ziglar

What this chapter tells you about Everlasting Employability:

- What you can learn from positive psychology.
- That you need to be in peak condition to generate peak performance.
- Always research and rehearse.
- The 10 things you need to do when meeting a prospective employer.
- How to be the best candidate at the interview.

Positive psychology is the science of the positive aspects of human life, such as well-being and flourishing. It was summarised in the words of its founder, Martin Seligman, as the *"scientific study of optimal human functioning [that] aims to discover and promote the factors that allow individuals and communities to thrive"*. In other words, it's about accentuating the positive.

Studies by experts in Positive Psychology think that there are a number of factors which make people happy and interestingly, research suggests that the happiest people are those that have discovered their personal strengths (such as persistence and critical thinking) and virtues (such as humanity or justice) and use those strengths and virtues for a greater purpose. So if you have completed the first half of this book then you are more than half way there! In addition, when we are involved in trying to reach a goal or in an activity that is challenging but well suited to our skills, we experience a joyful state called "flow."

With regards to interviewing technique it stands to reason that you need to project confidence that not only can you do the job, but that you are the best candidate. People often mirror what you project. If you are not confident, then your interviewer may have doubts too. To some extent, personality plays a part in how you project, as do experience, situation and mood swings. If you have had 10 straight rejections in a row then you may not be feeling at your most confident. All this may mean however is that you need to reconsider your targeting or your interview technique! As Henry Ford said: *"Failure is simply an opportunity to begin again, this time more intelligently."* No need to be a pessimist!

Winston Churchill once said: *"A pessimist sees the difficulty in every opportunity; an optimist sees the opportunity in every difficulty."* Clearly this is a continuum and many pessimists might simply consider themselves realistic. To be successful at interview however, you have to be a good salesman and that takes optimism.

Martin Seligman defines optimism as reacting to problems with a sense of confidence and high personal ability. Specifically, optimistic people believe that negative events are temporary, limited in scope (instead of pervading every aspect of a person's life), and manageable. Best of all however, is the evidence suggesting optimism is a learnable skill.

So you must be in the right frame of mind when you start interviewing. Prepare and script your sales pitch and market yourself as a premium product.

Henry Ford claimed that *"Whether you think you can, or think you can't, you're probably right."* In other words you have to believe in yourself.

So, when you are preparing your pitch, you need to use the "third chair" perspective. See yourself as others see you. Look back to that exercise on Reflected Best Self and remind yourself of all that you are great at.

Nigel Risner, a motivational speaker, has several loose leaf folders containing notes and pictures of achievements. Before he goes on stage he flicks through them to remind himself of all that he has achieved and give himself confidence. As humans we are programmed to recall our mistakes more easily than our successes, something that was needed for our survival. If you ask someone (outside a job interview) to recall an instance where they "failed"- in itself emotive language - he or she will often have every detail engraved on their heart. They will know what time it was, what they were wearing. Ask again to recount a success and people can barely recall one- let alone a whole loose leaf folder full! So it pays to give this some serious thought and consider all areas of your life: Climbing a mountain, being a good parent, passing a driving test, helping a colleague. You'll soon have two pages!

So the secret to a good performance at interview is preparation and you must be positive. An interview is an audition. You need to project yourself as the sort of the person the interviewer wants to hire. You have to come across as someone they want on the team. Show a little spark, show a little inspiration. Visualise stepping onto the pitch; think about the David Beckham story that was quoted earlier. When you come out of the dressing room it's your chance to shine.

Elite athletes can't do their best all of the time so they build up impetus for each big event and then wind down. So every now and then take a day off, do something different to recharge your batteries and find some new inspiration. You'll get stale otherwise and you have got to be on peak form when an important interview comes up.

Also be good to yourself. Wear a new suit to give yourself an edge. Or, if not a new suit, something new or loved - cufflinks, or a favourite tie. Buy clothes that make you feel like doing a little dance, that make you feel good about yourself. You'll love wearing them and it will show.

Research for success

When you get an interview, do your prep. It sounds obvious as everyone tells you to research. But it's not just a question of researching the organisation. You need to understand your interviewer and why he is hiring. One way or another he is looking for a solution to a problem. Just checking out the company's website and report and accounts is not enough. It's easy to find detailed information about potential employers online.

Having said that, you do need to check the company's website and annual report. Visit the website, take a good look at it and check out the tiny links at the bottom of the page for hidden corporate information.

Get the annual report (which includes the financials) –a lot of companies publish these on their websites. Where there is limited information available you can use the Companies House website, where it's very inexpensive to download company accounts. r Also use the many resources at your local reference library or call-in a favour. If you're a good networker you shouldn't have too much trouble getting help with some of this information when you need it.

Set-up Google alerts on your target companies so you can check breaking news. Search them out on Twitter and other social media sites so you understand their social media presence.

Work on understanding the needs of the organisation, look for opportunities and where you can add value. Look at the challenges and opportunities they face; work out how to show that your experience and expertise are relevant. Explore their marketplace, competitors and the changes taking place in the industry sector concerned.

Use your network to find information about the interviewer and his preferences, the company and its culture. Check social media sites as we suggested such as LinkedIn, ZoomInfo and Facebook to amass all the intelligence you can.

Rehearse your presentation

By this I don't necessarily mean any formal dialogue. I'm talking about what you say when anyone asks you what you do, why you may have left a company, what you have achieved and so on.

Can you talk about yourself comfortably, with confidence, concisely with clarity? Practice so that you have the right words, so that you don't go pink with embarrassment, so that you talk at the right pace and, crucially, know when to stop.

Practice some questions with someone you trust:

- Why did you leave your last job?
- Take me through your career history.
- Outline a major achievement in your last role.
- Tell me about a project that went wrong and why.
- What was your most difficult challenge as a manager?
- Tell me about what you do outside work.

You might be asked to talk about your social life. Be cautious. A salesman who is a cabaret artiste or a stuntman in his spare time may raise eyebrows.

If you got a new suit for the interview process that's a good move. You're worth it. Show potential employers that you're an attractive applicant with a positive, outgoing and flexible attitude to life.

Questions about your 'fit' are an important part of the job interview process. You need to be prepared to answer questions about yourself, your style of working, how you operate within a team, your strengths and weaknesses and possibly your views on topical issues.

Weaknesses are an area of questioning that can make you stop and think if you haven't prepared. Clearly you should have no weaknesses that would rule you out of the job. Think instead of development areas and skills that you would like to learn to help you progress into the next stage of your career.

Think about any questions you wouldn't want to be asked and rehearse your answers. Minimise anything negative and move to the positive. For example, if you are asked what your biggest mistake was, you might mention an historical incident briefly before saying what an important lesson you learnt from it. If you had a period of time off sick, you might be able to say that since the treatment you've not looked back.

Remember that you must absolutely not lie! Being "economical with the truth" is acceptable as long as it is not downright misleading. For example, if asked what you think of the management of a previous firm, you would employ tact in giving an appropriate answer if bad management style was the main reason you left.

Summary checklist: 10 things you must do
Remember: if you fail to prepare then prepare to fail.

1. Visit the website of the company you are going to see, take a good look at it and check out the tiny links at the bottom of the page for hidden corporate information.
2. Check out the LinkedIn and ZoomInfo profiles of the person you're meeting.
3. Get the financials – for all listed companies these will be available on the website, otherwise use Companies House, the resources at your local reference library or call-in a favour.
4. Call someone who has worked there or who knows them and get all the inside information you can about the firm and the person. Even

just a general idea of their style and culture will help you plan how to pitch yourself.

5. Check out the venue. Visit it so that you know exactly what your timing is to get there in good time. Look out for people coming and going to see what you can learn about the company culture. How are they dressed? Do they look happy?

6. Buy yourself something that will make you feel good and look professional. If you didn't get the new suit, get a new tie or a smart folder for your CV. Make sure your hair looks really good; a trip to a good hairdressers can do wonders for your confidence. Well cut, healthy, shiny hair is a must for an interview, and don't forget nails and shoes.

7. Write down and practice your elevator pitch and your exit statement. These sandwich your interview and are the entrance and the curtain call of your audition.

8. Swot up on the challenges that the organisation faces. Think about the opportunities presented and what is needed to exploit those opportunities. Then explore in the interview how you can help.

9. Find at least one thing that you have in common with the person you meet. Humans are simple enough; we tend to like people who are like us and we like people who like us. So find some common ground and it should work both ways.

10. Visualise success. It won't necessarily get you the job, because if it were as easy as just thinking about it, you wouldn't need advice. But it will give an edge to your performance. They want to hire a winner. You need to come across as a successful, proactive, flexible, thoughtful, "useful person to have about the place" candidate as well as being competent and qualified.

Chapter 11

The interview performance

"I am the greatest! I said that before I even knew I was."
                                                              Muhammad Ali

What this chapter tells you about Everlasting Employability:

- Why interviews are very imprecise tools.
- The rules of the interview game.
- Telling interviewers what you want them to know.
- Using body language to build rapport.
- Model answers to competency- based interviews.
- What really smart candidates do following an interview.

The truth about interviews is that there is a great deal of evidence to show that interview performance, on its own, is not a good predictor of successful job performance. The correlation of success at interview to successful job performance is only a factor of about 0.3. This does rise to 0.6 when an assessment centre is used. In other words, interviews are generally an imprecise art. Interviewers find it hard to be totally objective and can be impressed by someone who is simply good at interviews. Organisations often don't pick the best candidate for the job.

If you were offered the opportunity to invest £100k but "Oh, there's only a 30% chance of you getting a proper return on that investment" would you take the risk? Probably not, but organisations spend hours and much money on hiring. The good news for candidates is that most organisations are not that clever at recruiting. Often, hiring managers are not given much if any interview training. So just by reading this book you are going to be smarter than most interviewers. You are the smart candidate.

No matter what you might think, hiring good people is still one of the most difficult of business management tasks. Unfortunately most people talk themselves out of a job rather than talk themselves into it, through poor preparation or lack of confidence.

"My strengths? I'm especially good at answering the typical job interview questions. My weaknesses? I don't really like working."

So look back to what we said about Personal Brand and keep in mind the important research conducted by Professor Albert Mehrabian into how we take in information. He concluded that 55% of the information we take in is visual. The tone of what we say (i.e. how it sounds), makes up about 30% and only about 7% of what we actually say (the content) stays with the listener for any length of time. So it's not just what you wear but how you move and how you sound. For example, if you are asked a difficult question and you shift in your chair as you consider your answer, this can be an alarm signal to the interviewer to listen carefully to what comes next! Speaking quickly can be the sign of a quick mind, but it can also be interpreted as being nervous.

Bear in mind the truism that you only get one chance to make a first impression. The first three minutes of the interview are very important. Don't be remembered as the candidate who was late, who sat in the wrong chair or had chipped nail polish. If you make a good start then hopefully things will go really well and should even get better.

It's really hard to recover and do a good interview if you make a bad start. So at the heart of being a good interviewee is the key technique of establishing rapport. This is why you need to do your research and if at all possible find out what you have in common with the person you are going to meet.

The most effective way to start a meeting well is to smile. It sounds simple but it is disarmingly effective. Be a happy person, the sort of person people want to work with. If through humour you can establish rapport that's good, but be careful as a joke that falls flat is a bad beginning.

Think about all the adjectives to describe the right person for this job and how that person might project them: upbeat? energetic? positive? professional? capable? If you can be that person you will build rapport more quickly. You should think about what small talk you might engage in as you walk from the reception to the interview room. If the interviewer says nothing, then you can be proactive and try a positive comment about their offices or tell them something that you have found out through your research and how impressed you are. Flattery will take you a long way but take care not to overdo it. Don't be obsequious, just politely pleasant and come across as someone they want to know better.

In an interview you have to know your CV by heart. Ideally you should never in an interview have to say something you have not rehearsed. In fact a good interviewee has learned his or her lines in advance and is focussing much more on delivery than on off the cuff replies.

Achievements, failures, difficult tasks, things you are proud of, project successes and project failures, what you have learned along the way - all this you have prepared. None of it is pops into your head at the last minute; you know what you are going to say and what spin you are going to put on it.

What you really need to do, though, is to make it interactive! People trained in interview techniques are told to use the 70/30 rule. That means the interviewer should talk for about 30% of the time allotted and get the candidate to talk for 70% of the time in response.

The smart candidate actually wants a 50/50 dialogue. As the smart candidate, you will aim for a conversation directed along the lines you prefer – then you can play to your strengths.

The interviewer can only go with what you give them. This is best illustrated by using the "what was your biggest business mistake?" question. Do you really want to tell them your biggest mistake? Really? You decide!

So choose, for your answer, something that puts you in a favourable light. Say, for instance, that you don't know when to give up. It's a fault but it's a good fault to have in the greater scheme of things! And, you're aware of it and honest, so you try hard not to trip yourself up. It's a winning fault, in fact.

If you don't tell them that you lost £1m for your first employer then they can't go there. I'm not saying that you should be dishonest and if they know that you lost millions then you have to be able to explain that too, but the same rule applies - be judicious about what you choose to disclose.

The interactive interview is really important. Make it easy for the interviewer by saying "Have I told you all you need to know on that subject? Can I give you more detail?"

It's the way you tell 'em!
To increase the effectiveness of what you say, considering that they are likely to only remember part of what you tell them, talk in threes. Three things you remember, three achievements, three things you like. If it's a complex issue break it down into three stages. Threes are memorable.

Use sound bites and think about talking to the 3 to 5 minute rule. Don't monopolise the conversation, you want it to be two-way. Don't witter. Also don't ever, ever, say "to be honest with you" because the sub-text is that you aren't always honest.

Consider pitch and pace in your delivery too. Vary your delivery to maintain interest. Listen to presenters on television for tips on how to make the way you sound more engaging. Some newsreaders make the news sound really interesting and don't drone. Slow down on points of particular importance so that they register, speed up in between and use emphasis on key words. That way the interviewer's brain will register interest and they'll keep with you. Content isn't enough on its own.

But remember it's not a monologue. You are both actors in this interview and it is a dialogue, a conversation, not a solo performance. Watch for signals from the other side of the table. Check the attention level and responses of the interviewer frequently. Remember most people can't concentrate for more than 10 minutes at a time and a lot of people for rather less time than that. If you have lost their attention you'll spot the glazed look or the fidget.

Remember that some HR practitioners are interviewing all day long so it's not really surprising if their attention wanders when a candidate is repetitive, or plain boring. If you interview six people a day, by the end the day it's pretty hard to remember one from the other unless you really like something or really hate something about one of them. Recommendations to go forward may rest on that sort of impression, so make sure you're a good interviewee.

Body language (i.e. eye contact, posture and gesture) is important. We know that the information we take in is, by and large, visual information – so how we appear in terms of body language is critical.

Eye contact

One way to establish rapport and show engagement is in how we physically relate to another person. Look them in the eye. The "rule" in British culture is to maintain constant eye contact when the other person is talking to show you are listening with rapt attention. The person that is doing the talking looks directly at the listener then will glance away while they gather their next thought. Don't stare endlessly, but if you want to make a very significant point or emphasise a point or re-engage their attention then keep eye contact. It's OK to look towards the ceiling when asked a question if you need to think about your answer, as that is where most people look when they are trying to recall information. It means that you are thinking about your answer - it's not off pat - and will therefore tend to make you look genuine. However, don't look down at your boots, particularly if it's a question around integrity or any such issue. It's thought that people tend to look down when they are trying to manufacture an answer, which could then be interpreted as an untruth! However different cultures have different ways of doing things. Asian women naturally appear to look down more, perhaps because it is considered polite.

Body posture

Your posture should be appropriate. Sitting tall as though you have a piece of string pulling you up from the top of your head will make you look confident and alert. However, sitting back with your hands behind your head is often taken as a strong indication that you are over-confident. This would look arrogant to some whereas you want to look business-like. Similarly, sitting forward with your hands in a praying position might make you look meek, anxious even.

Don't worry about gesturing; with occasional use it can be very effective to make a point. But beware of over doing it as it may become distracting. The colourful British Scientist, Dr Magnus Pyke, used excessive hand movements on his television appearances which, whilst entertaining, often meant that you missed the point of his talk!

Then there's mirroring – look at how your interviewer is sitting, and in such a way that he or she doesn't notice what you are doing, mirror their actions. This way good rapport happens naturally.

So you need to be aware of the interviewers' attention level and their body language. Switch position every now and then. When you cross your legs you tend to attract a higher level of attention at that moment.

So try to think about the person on the other side of the table and how much you look like them and behave like them. We hire people like us and people we like. We struggle to hire those who are very different from us.

That's why diversity is such a difficult issue in the workplace. We tend to hire clones of ourselves or people we have hired in the past whom we have liked or who were successful. We like to try to replicate what worked before.

Candidate assessment techniques
Increasingly organisations are using competency-based assessment and structured interviewing. Put simply, they are trying to understand more

objectively what it was you did, what skills you used and what knowledge you applied so they can then focus on the outcomes achieved. Your interview brief should tell you what competencies are being tested for so that you can consider examples which can demonstrate your prowess.

In response, a good structure to use is the STAR model with an added L at end. So you are going to be talking in terms of:

- What was the **S**ituation?
- What was the **T**ask?
- What **A**ction did you take?
- What were the **R**esults?
- AND, in addition, what did you **L**earn from the situation?

Then there is the CIDS interview which stands for Chronological In Depth Structured interview. This is an interview style that focuses on top grading. Developed by consultant Bradford Smart of TopGrading.com, it involves focused questions covering 50 competencies in six categories. These comprise: intellectual, personal, interpersonal, management, leadership and motivational.

In his book, *Topgrading*, Smart states that any organization can use topgrading to weed out underachievers and focus on "A" players. By avoiding the often-used scattergun question technique, interviewers instead *"probe the patterns of how this person developed competencies throughout his career."* You may be asked to answer numerous questions about every job you have ever had coupled with extensive background checking. The process can take up to 6 months.

The Gallup Interview is tailored to particular jobs or occupations. Rather than focusing on what's wrong with people, Gallup looks at success and tries to understand what makes it happen. They've found that successful people talk and think differently from average or low performers.

Everyone has consistent, recurring patterns of thoughts, feelings and behaviour. Gallup calls these patterns 'life themes'. The technique tries to draw these out of you and weigh them against key competencies needed in the role you're interested in.

If you've followed my advice about career MOT, skills audit and career planning, you should be well prepared for these sorts of approach.

You don't always have to talk about successes. You can discuss a failure too, so long as you can show what you have learned from it. Always being able to learn from what you do is a crucial skill.

Again, good candidates who have lots of self-awareness seek out positive feedback because they are in continuous improvement mode. You want to improve your interview technique so any feedback you can get will help and, as we said before, take notes on things you did well and things you can learn from for next time.

You need to have a closing statement prepared to say why you are interested in the company and what you can do for them. Show them how you will add value. Think about what you can tell them about yourself or the sector that will help them do their job better.

While you may not like it, you do need to have an answer to the question "Why are you the best candidate?" Now is no time to be modest but a short answer is indicated.

Always be grateful. Irrespective of the outcome, tell your interviewer how glad you are to have had the opportunity to meet them.

Becoming an exceptional candidate is something you can do. Most people don't take the trouble.

After the meeting

As soon as you get out of the interview, take a break. Write down what you heard and everything you can remember. An interview is an opportunity to learn more about you. Make some notes about how you felt each interview went as soon as possible afterwards. If there were some aspects that you found awkward, concentrate on practicing your responses for next time.

If you have managed a 50/50 conversational interview you will have soaked up a mass of information. Try to capture as much as you. What did they say when you asked about the challenges?

Within 48 hours you should send them a one or two page letter, a "leave-behind" which reflects what you heard around the challenges and opportunities and links to your experience, showing how you can add value. A "leave-behind" document gets passed around. One person rarely makes the decision to hire in isolation. The recruiter will seek validation of their decision and the "leave-behind" is something that can be passed around when they ask "What do you think?" So a tailor-made statement from you is invaluable.

To my mind this is much more important than your CV. If you have listened efficiently then you should be able to reflect back what you have been told. And people like being told what they have told you.

After every interview, make time for a period of reflection. If you can get feedback then ask for it. Look at what went well and focus on that. Don't get hung up on what didn't work. Review anything you can improve on. Going forward you should concentrate on what you do well and do more of it.

In summary, remember that interviews are an imprecise science and that the prepared candidate will always out-perform the unprepared candidate.

Since most of the information we take in is visual, presentation is key. So use body language and eye contact to build up rapport and keep your interviewer with you by pacing your presentation- speed up, slow down and use intonation and emphasis wisely. Don't drone on!

Prepare lots of examples to demonstrate your skills, knowledge and achievements using the STAR (L) model for competency based questions. Don't forget the rule of three!

Remind yourself just how much you have to offer, so stay calm, be confident and smile!

Finally, don't forget to follow up the interview with a "leave-behind".

Chapter 12

The inevitable chapter on writing a CV

"Boxing was the only career where I wouldn't have to start out at the bottom. I had a good resume".

Sugar Ray Leonard

The traditional view as supported by Linda is that CVs are very important in a job search and people should spend a lot of time tailoring them. Michael's view is that they are increasingly less relevant in job searching today. The advent of LinkedIn and other social media makes them less relevant. The proactive job search model places much more importance on getting recommendations as a way of getting into organisations. That said, we both agree that if you produce a CV then it has to be a good marketing tool, well presented and grammatically correct.

What this chapter tells you about Everlasting Employability:

- CVs are an important tool in helping you to get a job interview - not a job.
- You need your CV to stand out to make you memorable.
- Get feedback on your CV - it's a great way to build your network.

You need a CV that works for you. It is your marketing document but you should be aware that the average recruiter is likely to spend no more than 2-3 minutes reading it. Recruiters spend most time looking at your current job (job title and length of time you were in post), the previous one and then your education. In my experience most people who interview other people for jobs look at the CV on the way to the interview room.

As a result, I believe that there is an over-emphasis on the importance of the CV. Jobseekers spend hours redefining, refreshing and rewriting their

CVs. I don't want you to feel cheated and if you bought this book I know you will want to polish your CV.

However the good thing about spending time on a CV is that it will focus your mind on your skills and achievements – it is a useful way to remind yourself of these in advance of those networking and interview meetings. Networking and getting in front of the relevant "point of purchase" person is your No.1 priority. In the proactive career management model of job seeking, the CV is less important than a good leave-behind.

In terms of CV design, what this means is that writing a good CV comes down to form not function - it is more a question of format than content.

A CV is never a single, finalised, document. It is an organic document that grows with you. So you need to review it at least every year immediately following your Career MOT.

A CV should always be tailored for a particular organisation or a particular job. Make sure you adjust the profile to reflect the role you are applying for and you may need to adjust your achievements to reflect the needs of the organisation or role.

Having said that, you should always have a CV ready. So although I tried to convince you that it is not really important, here are all the things you need to know about a good CV.

A marketing document needs to be eye-catching but for the right reasons. All too often the wrong reasons are bad spelling and grammar! You'd be surprised how many people go to grammar school but can't spell the word grammar.

Likewise the English spelling of the word "liaise" trips up many people, as does the difference between "led" and "lead". You can't rely entirely on the spellcheck function.

Write it from the perspective of the person reading it and also the search engines that are going to look for key words in it.

Help recruiters by making the CV easy to read. This is so that they can pigeonhole you - that's how they work. In the appendices you will find a template to help you. An outline sequential of the key elements might look like this:

Start with a profile. This will catch the eye and tell people where you have come from, where you are going, what you are looking for. At all costs avoid words like dynamic, ambitious, creative – there is no way you can prove those things. Make the profile a factual statement.

Your previous experience should be listed next, in reverse chronological order from the most recent role. Recruiters are only interested in the last 10 years. Focus on outputs which are quantitative. Process (i.e. what drove outputs) is less important.

You might need to include a brief positioning statement – what the job was and where it sat in the organisation. Avoid in-house jargon – EMC, DivMD, etc.

Tell it as a journey - a successful one. Arrange your achievements to reflect the importance of these relative to the organisation or role you are applying for. The last 10 years are the important ones. Beyond that just list the company name and your job title unless there is something that you really feel is important to emphasise. They can ask if they need to know more.

Now for the tricky bit - the part that really distinguishes the excellent candidate from the average one. If you listed your achievements you have probably reached the second page. If the interviewer is still reading then you have caught their interest but what you have to do next is take that to another level.

You need to say something memorable about yourself to spark an interest in arranging to meet you. So, for example, I remember from outplacement client CVs

- a Lloyds broker who worked as part of Tony Blair's delegation to China,
- a marketing guy who was responsible for the introduction of Fosters lager with the Paul Hogan adverts, and
- a Finance Director looking for move into general management role who had no marketing experience. He had, however, worked actively for a small charity as flag-day salesman, then as treasurer and eventually as chairman of trustees and there had been significant revenue growth under his aegis.

Something like this quoted in your CV is really useful. This is the page where you name-drop people you know or have worked with. You can use your life outside work. If you have done work for a trade association, have been published or undertaken public speaking engagements, mention them here.

On the lighter side I remember one person saying that in his own time he wrestled alligators. It was a joke to get him noticed and not a technique I would normally recommend. But weigh up whether you are getting attention for the right reasons. Most people find this the most difficult part to complete so think long and hard.

Hobbies say a lot about people, for example stamp collecting and marathon running might suggest you are a loner. Don't list the theatre as a hobby unless you are prepared to talk intelligently about the last play you saw. Being able to play an instrument is by contrast something that takes a great deal of talent and tenacity and often commands respect.

The length of your CV is a matter of discretion – it doesn't have to be one page of A4 but it absolutely cannot be 15 pages. It should be designed to sell you as an individual so I would expect a research analyst to go into some detail reflecting varied or specific research capability whereas a City trader might get a CV onto one page. There is no fixed rule.

The next section is qualifications. Give the highest level of qualification you have. If you have a degree then you don't need to list all your O and A levels or your cycling proficiency certificate. But language A levels add an extra element to your skill-set even where the job may not specifically need them. That's all there is to it.

Don't forget your contact details, preferably at the top of the page. Make it easy to read and easy to find out how to get hold of you. Your mobile number is very important. Don't have a juvenile email address – hotbabe@hotmail is not going to make a good impression. Equally something obscure such as mdm136@gmail is not memorable and won't be easy to find in an Outlook address drop-down. Your email address should be name-based. And why not add your LinkedIn profile URL for added colour?

Which is the most boring font? Times New Roman? You will find a wide choice of fonts and proportional spacing on your PC. Experiment and see what looks best but bear in mind that clean fonts without serifs (the extra twiddly bits) are much easier to read on screen and on the page. Also, some more obscure fonts are not supported on all computers.

If you are emailing or attaching your CV to an application, always send it in PDF form. According to Sod's Law, a Word CV will always print differently through someone else's PC and printer and all the time you spent making it look right will be wasted. Carefully lined-up dates will no longer line-up, headings will be left sitting in splendid isolation at the foot of a page and your strategically placed page-break will generate a nice blank page in the middle of your printed CV. PDF converters are available free on the internet and some can be used without downloading any software. With a PDF, WYSIWYG – what you see is what you get.

If you want a really professional looking document, take the time to find out how to set and use the tabs and possibly also the tables in your word processing package. It usually shows when a CV writer has been hitting the space bar like a mad man in the hope that a column of dates will line up – because when printed they don't. Someone in your office will know about these things and be happy to show you.

So you should spend more time thinking about layout than the content. Job done. Don't spend too much time on it - get networking.

Incidentally, it's good to ask for an opinion from your network on your CV when it's appropriate. But don't take on board all the feedback unless it is really consistent. After all if you ask 10 people for their opinions, you'll get 10 opinions. You decide what makes sense.

Likewise, if you ask a career coach or recruiter about CV format you'll get a different answer from each of them. There is no right way to write a CV but what is really important is that you are happy with it and it reflects your brand and is what you might call "fit for purpose".

In summary:

- Your CV is a marketing document.
- Concentrate on more form than content.
- Focus on quantifiable achievements not tasks.
- Say something different or interesting about yourself, your brand or what is remarkable about you.

Remember: The CV is just one of a number of tools available to market you. Your network of contacts and how you work it is what you should concentrate on.

Part 3

Back to the future

Chapter 13

So you've just been made redundant!

"I didn't see it then, but it turned out that getting fired from Apple was the best thing that could have ever happened to me. The heaviness of being successful was replaced by the lightness of being a beginner again, less sure about everything. It freed me to enter one of the most creative periods of my life."

Steve Jobs, (1955-2011) Co-Founder, Chairman, and CEO of Apple Inc. (fired in 1986; re-hired in 1996), and former CEO of Pixar

What this chapter tells you about Everlasting Employability:

- How to ride the roller-coaster of change.
- Focusing on your achievements, both now and in the past.
- How you build resilience.
- Getting on-message.

So let's consider the psychology of rejection. Are you a different person? Of course not! You have the same talents, the same skills and though it's hard, you have to distance yourself from the fact that you have just been rejected.

Remind yourself of all your achievements, of what you are good at, and what things people say about you. Angry? You bet! Shocked, depressed or frustrated? Probably.

You may experience some or all of the stages associated with grieving. Elizabeth Kubler-Ross, during her work with people undergoing grief and bereavement, developed a model identifying the process involved in coping with major life changes.

Redundancy is a major life change, like moving house or divorce. The initial shock of redundancy gives way to anger and loss of self-confidence before you are able to start making decisions and changes.

The following stages are typical of the change curve which you may recognise if you've experienced major change.

1. Shock and surprise at the announcement.
2. Denial of the change, convincing yourself and others that it isn't really happening or won't make any difference to you.
3. Frustration and anger, often with a tendency to blame others.
4. Depression and apathy, everything seems pointless and purposeless.
5. Experimentation where you are able to try new things out.
6. Coming to terms with what's happened and starting to feel more optimistic and positive.
7. Integrating the changes into your life.

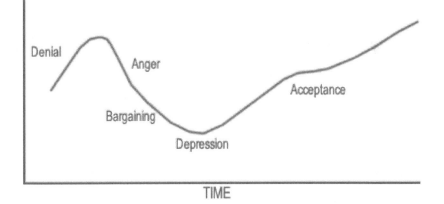

It's normal to go through these emotions. It's important to recognise and deal with them so as to take control and move on.

There's no defined timescale for how long it takes to work through the process but recognising where you are on the curve helps. We're all different and there's no way to know how long it will take you to work through each stage. It might be one day or six months.

What not to do:

- Panic.
- Call headhunters.
- Circulate a hastily drawn up CV.
- Bad-mouth your former employer.

You need to focus on yourself, not obsessively so but take some time to decide the right course of action and to prioritise your objectives for job search. Rudyard Kipling advises us to "*meet with Triumph and Disaster, and treat those two impostors just the same*". Don't let redundancy damage your self-confidence. We know that success in the search for a new job is more likely if you have good levels of confidence and self-esteem.

Life throws brickbats at us every so often, but something better may be just around the corner. Be prepared to succeed. In fact, be a Boy Scout, be prepared.

Focus on how you are going to sell your unique brand of skills and experience.

Now read your CV and see if you can improve it since you last updated it. This is the time to focus on your successes and achievements.

Exercise

1. List your top three achievements.
2. Now list three more.
3. And another three; have you dried up yet? If not, then carry on listing.

Most people run out of things to list after six or nine. They concentrate on major achievements and recent achievements. But remember what we said about Nigel Risner earlier and his loose-leaf file full of achievements. All of your achievements, little and large, are valid in the context of this review. Successes from your personal life, your academic record or sporting achievements, the time you won Salesperson of the Month in your part-time job that helped you through university or college. All valid.

We focus on our big successes and most recent achievements and tend to discount previous achievements. Don't discount them; they made you what you are. You may not list them all on your CV but for the purposes of reviewing your career to date and updating the CV, give yourself a pat on the back.

When we were little we were given badges in the Cubs and Brownies and we wore them with pride. We proudly posted certificates and rosettes on the bedroom wall. As we get older we dismiss these achievements. What was once all-consuming, for instance your O and A levels, are now a distant memory, though at the time they were mountains you successfully climbed.

Revisit all your achievements. Celebrating your achievements builds confidence and self-belief. The power of the self-fulfilling prophecy is astonishing. Use the Best Reflected Self exercise that we suggested in the Career MOT section, Chapter 3. There's a form you can use in the Appendix. The good thing about this exercise is that it makes you aware of things that other people think are important about you. Very often there are things you take for granted, that others recognise and value.

Remember: things don't always turn out the way we plan. Everyone has setbacks and sometimes they can weigh heavily, but it doesn't mean the end of the world. Even if you fear you may have made a mistake or a misjudgement - well we all make mistakes on occasion - that's how we learn and grow. It's how you deal with it that matters. Reading Steve Jobs' biography is interesting. Being voted off the board of the company he founded was a defining moment in his career.

So we can't get on with everyone. We can't control everything. Sometimes we are just in the wrong place at the wrong time. It's about learning lessons and moving on. Are you still on the platform or on the train? Take a deep breath, push out negative feelings and think about what you can control in the future.

Try to be resilient when faced with adversity. Not everybody is going to love you or your work. Sometimes things just don't work out the way you planned. It happens. Expand your horizons and learn to deal with the unexpected. It's just like following the England football team. Don't stop taking the penalties just because we lose shoot–outs!

Build resilience

Successful people are resilient. They bounce back from failure. Entrepreneurs have a mind-set that doesn't accept failure as something to worry about. Failure happens. Pick yourself up and address the next project.

Remember the legend of Robert the Bruce and the spider. Robert I, King of Scotland, after six successive defeats by the English armies, was a fugitive in a damp and lonely cave. Bruce was at the lowest point of his life. He thought about leaving the country and never coming back.

He watched a spider try to build a web in the cave entrance and succeed on the seventh try. Bruce took courage from the spider's perseverance, fought a seventh time, and won.

This is a story my mother used to tell me to teach me resilience and fortitude. I was asthmatic as a child and was often upset and frustrated when I was kept off school and missed things I wanted to do.

Take stock. Decide what you need to do next, always accentuating the positives. The easy job search is where you are looking for employment using the same skills in the same industry. Focus on the competitors of your previous employer. Turn to the section on proactive job search.

Look at your finances. Do some calculations and see where you stand. How much time have you got before the money runs out? Create a cash flow. Seek out financial advice. Don't take the entire load on yourself, share it with a spouse, or someone you trust, and look at where you can make savings.

And it's important to take some time out in order to refresh yourself. Reconsider your plan. Revisit the work you've done earlier on strengths, skills, achievements and values. Look at your options. Are there new options that occur to you now or is this the golden opportunity to do something you have long dreamt of doing?

Previously you will have considered your elevator pitch. Consider if you will have to change this in any way. You will know what feels comfortable for you to say in your own words but, for example, if you are asked directly what your current employment situation is you might say something along the lines of "I'm currently on garden leave as the company restructured recently as you may have heard. But I'd been there for 5 years during which time I learnt/handled a new project/ completed a large transaction. As a result I feel ready to move on to a new challenge." Make sure your delivery is upbeat and positive - after all, you've got talent! Practice in front of the bathroom mirror, telling yourself that you are the best candidate for this role. Keep it simple, keep it honest.

Make sure you can describe your career as a journey with a destination. Get this scripted to your satisfaction. Not more than five or so sentences that tell who you are and where you're going.

Remember how important it is to focus on how you deliver it – not on what you say but how you say it. If you are lacking confidence, try not to show it. If you feel down because you have been selected for redundancy, there is a danger that a negative attitude can translate into a negative performance at interview.

You have to be like an actor and learn your lines. You must sound convincing, so focus on delivery and remember that there has to be congruence between what you say and your body language. Practice with a trusted advisor or mentor.

Remember the importance of your network. It's important to start making contact with those who can help you. Re-surface quickly, be seen, and be positive.

Review the chapter on networking and think of networking in terms of a balance sheet. Networking is about adding value to your network –if you have been doing it right you will be in credit, so now is the time to make a withdrawal.

If you had problems with the boss in your last job, someone you just couldn't get on with, consider that this may not be down to you. Some people are just unreasonable or worse! Typically we blame ourselves and allow this to undermine our confidence. We already know that when you lack confidence your performance suffers.

You should reflect on what you contributed to the failure of the relationship but just because he, or she, was the boss it doesn't necessarily follow that he, or she, was right and you were wrong. Sometimes bosses are unreasonable.

A lot of people think they can manage their boss, but there are some people you just can't manage. If you really are working with someone of that nature it's probably better to get out. The boss is not likely to change his, or her, ways.

If you spend a long time working for a poor boss it can damage you. In hostage situations this is known as the "Stockholm syndrome" where you bond with someone who treats you badly. It's a way of dealing with a difficult situation but it's not a way to work long term.

However, we all know that people can be unreasonable. Life is not fair. Get over it and move on. Don't blame yourself, don't look for answers. Park it and get on with life.

In summary:

- Focus on your achievements.
- Work out your elevator pitch and your exit statement.
- Get networking.
- Use the proactive job search model.
- Get on the train and off the platform
- Live the rest of your life

Chapter 14

Second and third careers

"It is never too late to be what you might have been."

George Eliot

We have the paradigm that at 65 years of age we should retire. This is manifestly not the case. You have the capability to continue working beyond that age and increasingly we will need to. This chapter is all about this new paradigm.

What this chapter tells you about Everlasting Employability:

- A new work paradigm: funding our pension.
- You might have to work but you have choices.
- Working when you want to work, working when you want to get paid.

Plan your career cycle. It used to be that we expected to move through a series of jobs and then retire. These days, though, we are likely to gravitate from a full-time job to a portfolio career. We'll hope to work when we want to, probably not for an employer but on a freelance or contract basis, with time to do other things that interest us.

Consider what you want to be working on when you are in your 40s, 50s, 60s and maybe your 70s. Think about life after full-time work and what your portfolio of options might look like.

Hitting 50 can herald a sea change for many. There tends to be a shift from having to work for a living to doing work that has real personal meaning and value. You may need flexibility to fit with family commitments. Personal and professional life are parallel and need to be in sync, so perhaps a portfolio career or freelance work may help you balance lifestyle needs with career priorities.

Between 40 and 60 you must start thinking about what sort of work you want to concentrate on. A portfolio of career, freelance roles, voluntary work and personal development time is the aim of many. It's important to step back and take some time for yourself when you can. If you've always felt you should try something else or put something back into the community, perhaps you now have the time and willingness to make some lifestyle adjustments that will accommodate those aspirations.

So why am I talking about working after the age of 60? Well you need to think about what you are going to do when you finish full-time work. You may not want to finish work at 65. We're going to work on after we are 60 because most of us are going to live into our 80s and it's unlikely that our pension provisions alone will sustain us.

Retiring at 60 or 65 is part of an old paradigm based on fact that men died in their early 60s – the same old paradigm that had you working for one employer for your entire career on a full-time basis. There is now a rise in the number of self-employed people who are selling their service to a number of employers, including former employers.

The advantage to the employers is obvious – they have someone they know, with skills they are confident in but don't have to pay them all the time. They just pay them when they need them.

The advantage to the employee is that you work when you want to work and, more importantly, are not reliant on one source of income as you have a number of clients who will support you.

This is the portfolio career whereby you

- generate revenue from a number of sources,
- act on your desire to put something back, to create a better society, implement your personal CSR (Corporate Social Responsibility) policy, and
- spend time on yourself and what is important to you. That might be on more leisure but also it might be about learning and having fun.

What we know is that in the modern economy there is a business case for the flexible workforce. From a business perspective you only pay when you need the skills and from a personal perspective you only work when you want to work. This engenders an employer to employee relationship which is adult to adult and not parent to child.

The power of universal connectivity means that you don't necessarily have to be in the office to do what the organisation needs. So it's a very different business relationship - what you could call a symbiotic business relationship i.e. one with mutual benefits. The organisation wants variable cost and the ability to call up and stand down highly skilled individuals. Individuals want recognition, both financial and non-financial, as well as networking and development opportunities.

This latter point is really key because if you don't continually develop then ultimately you will be trying to sell a set of skills which are obsolete.

The rise of the interim manager is also a manifestation of the portfolio career concept. Interim contracts are popular for the same reason, because organisations want a flexible resource but also a highly qualified one.

Working this way means that as workers we need to grow a whole new set of skills – those that relate to being able to run our own business. If you are going to be working for several different organisations on a flexible basis it is not sufficient just to have skills the market wants to buy.

You will have to develop marketing skills so you can sell yourself and also build business administration capability in everything from knowing where to get stationery to arranging insurance and proper IT support. You will need to be your own accountant and manage your own credit control and pay VAT. I'm not saying this is necessarily a tough transition to make but conventional wisdom says that 80% of small businesses fail in the first 18 months. Working for yourself can be lonely and having to condense all the skills required in sales, marketing, finance and operations into one can be tough.

However, that is not my experience. What I know is that people who set up portfolio careers in their 30s and 40s achieve their income targets but it typically takes 18 months not 12. Variability of income and the lack of a social network is what portfolio workers most often comment on. Most people go out to work because they like meeting people.

More importantly, it's hard work when you end up doing VAT at the weekend - it's this sort of thing that can drive people back into full time employment.

Having said that, there are many organisations and accountants who specialise in supporting small (e.g. one-person) consultancies with company and VAT registration, corporation tax and company secretarial returns and general book-keeping. For a cost of about one day's fees a quarter, this can seem like excellent value. Also, VAT accounting may not be as daunting as you might think. HMRC operates what it calls the "flat-rate VAT scheme" for small businesses. This allows you to do away with accounting for VAT on your business expenses and so only have to worry about charging VAT to your customers.

If you try the self-employment route when you are in your 30s or 40s and end up going back into employment, that's no bad thing. You are a better business person for the experience you gained in running your own company and your CV has added depth. It's not failure if you give up, but an invaluable learning experience that builds on your development as a manager.

For those in their 50s and 60s, you have to see this paradigm as a new way of working. Organisations need to be increasingly flexible and people don't need to be in the office to do a job if they can do it remotely and perhaps not on a 9 to 5 basis.

It's important for employees going down this route to realise that they have to self-invest and to develop the skills they need to be a successful one--person business.

Early retirement is often not retirement at all but just a means of taking control and changing direction. Nowhere is it written that you can't start your own business at 65.

Alternative careers are also demanding on your ability to adjust, but you'll be making new connections, building new networks and if you are doing something really interesting and worthwhile, the rewards will be tangible if not so financially enticing. If you are planning a portfolio career you'll need new skills and to prepare by continuing to invest in yourself.

Remember your career plan is an on-going project. Don't get complacent, and keep asking how well your personal plan is working. If you can answer "just fine" then continue to keep an eye on potential career developments and changes in your professional field, and you will stay on track. If, or when, your answer becomes "no" or you're not sure, revisit your personal development plan.

Career time ticks away faster than you might think but remember it's never too late to reset the clock.

Chapter 15

Staying employed

"If you do what you love, you'll never work a day in your life."

Winston Churchill

What this chapter tells you about Everlasting Employability:

- The importance of a career plan.
- Building the right profile.
- The importance of continuous learning.
- Participate in life inside and outside the organisation.

© 2012 Ted Goff

"I have a funny feeling that you're going to tell me to do something, even though my schedule is completely full of not doing anything."

The secret of employability is pretty obvious really – it's about having a set of skills that the marketplace is willing to buy.

The dichotomy is that organisations typically only want to employ you for skills you have. When those skills are no longer relevant they will, in the nicest possible way, get rid of you. It's a very forward-thinking organisation that will train you up for a set of skills that you are going to need in the future.

So you have, as an individual, to understand the marketplace in which you operate. And you have to have a view as to where that market is going and the skills that are going to be sought-after in the future

The analogy to recall here is that of the Java programmer versus the VHS Video operator we referred to in Chapter 1.

So what can you do to ensure employability? The first and most important thing is have a clear, defined career plan. Then keep self-investing to keep your skills up to date. THIS IS NOT THE RESPONSIBILITY OF YOUR EMPLOYER - whatever they may say!

The old paradigm was that most people thought if they were good and loyal employees, kept their heads down and worked hard, the organisation would look after them. Nothing could be further from the truth.

Remember Boxer in Orwell's Animal Farm, the farm's most hard-working and loyal labourer. With his determination to be a good servant and his penchant for hard work, Boxer works tirelessly for the cause of Animal Farm, operating under his personal maxims, "I will work harder" and "Napoleon is always right."

His death shows how far the pigs are willing to go. When he collapses from overwork, the pigs say they have sent him to a veterinarian. In fact they have sent him to the knacker's yard to be slaughtered and rendered in exchange for money to buy a case of whisky for the pigs.

You are working for yourself.

So how do you develop these skills for the future? In part it's about making the right noises within the organisation. Do seek out personal development reviews and act on them. Do spend time with your manager and negotiate an individual contract whereby they know the skills you want to develop and you identify the skills they are prepared to invest in.

It's worth pointing out that off the job training (courses and business schools) is becoming less popular because it does not embed the learning in the same way that active learning models do. Learning has to bring a return on investment; there have to be demonstrable business benefits. Organisations are increasingly making use of real work projects as vehicles to embed learning and realise business benefits. This is often referred to as "the flipped classroom" and the groups of employees working together are referred to as Action Learning Sets. It is possible to deliver learning via technology, articles, videos, blogs and podcasts available globally online, 24/7. Participants can share learning, ideas and questions with their learning sets inside and outside the organisation. It is possible to poll participants, to discuss the messages delivered by the more established learning methods and generate online debate. It is important to understand in this new environment that whilst still delivering demonstrable benefits for the business, it is very much down to you to take responsibility for your own development. Yes some of this development will take place in work but increasingly it will take place in your own time. This is all about you investing in you.

Organisations are well aware that by investing in MBA training for example, often all they are doing is making the person more likely to leave the organisation. Although there is evidence to counter this view, it is how most managers still think.

Next make sure that within the organisation you are known for the right reason and right profile. This is so that you have people who will support your endeavours to get more training and more development.

Again, it's obvious, but if you are seen as a thorn in the side, the organisation will not support you. You always need friends in high places! Learn to manage upwards and make sure you are visible, not ubiquitous, just visible for all the right reasons. Visible because you are good at your job. Don't assume you will be recognised as a matter of course, that's not enough. Do a bit of self-promotion.

You need to commit your own personal time and this does mean giving up some weekends and evenings. It doesn't have to be expensive – e-learning, distance-based courses and the whole plethora of blended learning options are available cost-effectively these days.

One key competency to develop is that of curiosity, to be always asking "why?" and looking for connections and links. So be a reader. Be someone who does not just look inward but who looks outward too. Work on being useful to the organisation – the person who is "useful to have about the place". Be versatile and flexible – certain people always know things because they take the time and trouble to find out.

Get out and about in terms of professional associations. Have good networks, use LinkedIn and meet competitors. All these are sources of information and knowledge that you should accumulate and build on. Remember that employability is not just about where you are now but about staying current in the marketplace.

It's unrealistic to think that one employer will always be the employer for you. So what you need to have, in the event of them saying "thank you but no thank you", is the skills that any other employer would want.

Write down your personal development plan and re-contract with yourself each and every year. Check that you did what you said you were going to do and if you didn't, ask yourself why not? Remember what we said earlier about the correlation between writing down goals and achieving those goals.

Being curious and finding out about yourself is key – it is really important to seek feedback by actively looking for 360° reviews or by doing psychometric assessment.

It isn't reasonable to think that you will be using only one set of skills in one sector for your whole working life – obviously taking existing skills into a different sector is the second easiest way to get a new job. Your ability to achieve this is, needless to say, a function of how good and broad-based your network is.

Be a player, not just someone who watches from the sidelines. Volunteer for projects, particularly those to do with social corporate responsibility schemes, because, as already discussed, you learn fast in new environments.

Be a go-to person. Remember the old adage "if you want something done, ask a busy person". Some people never seem to be unemployed.

One final thing – don't be one of the starlings in the nest, always sitting there with mouth open expecting good things to come along. Get out there and find what you want and deserve.

In summary:

- Employability is about building a set of skills the marketplace needs.
- It's down to you.
- You need to continue to invest in building knowledge and skills.
- Get feedback.
- Be a player.

Chapter 16

Key learning points for Everlasting Employability

1. It's down to you. You are in control, maybe not of everything, but you can't sub-contract your career management to a third party.

2. You've got to have a plan, to know where you are going and how you are going to get there. Write it down.

3. Share your plan with your network and work on building that network. You do this by adding value to its members.

4. You have to work in a way that is structured and systematic, so build yourself a CRM database for your networking.

5. Proactively job search - target companies and use your network to get in front of the point of purchase.

6. Prepare for interviews – prepare, practise and use positive psychology.

7. Think laterally, out of the box, and not always upward - use your imagination.

8. It's not about the job. It's about a career that matches your life-cycle phases and about long-term employability.

9. Concentrate on self-investment and continuous learning.

10. No one is more important than you. The only thing holding you back is you.

11. You need to think for the future or move away from the old paradigm of one career and one job. You are going to need to move between jobs and be in a position to be self-employed in a portfolio career in your 60s.

Appendices

Appendix 1

CV template

[Full Name]

Address:

Email:

Mobile telephone Number:

PERSONAL PROFILE

Insert a profile paragraph about you. Tell me where you have come from by way of experience and your intended destination.

MOST SIGNIFICANT ACHIEVEMENTS

Highlight where you feel you have added most value to the organisations you have worked for. Relate to the challenges and opportunities faced by the organisation to which you are applying.

KEY SKILLS

These must correlate to the organisation's requirements.

WORK HISTORY

Only highlight the last ten years.

Company name   **Dates**

Short business description.

Responsibilities

List the key 4 or 5 things that you were responsible for (your duties).

This can include your position within the organisation and to whom you reported if appropriate.

Achievements

List the most important things you achieved in your role (what you made happen). Highlight the quantifiable benefits or outcomes.

YOUR UNIQUE SELLING POINTS

Assuming you are now half way down page two, you can assume the reader has an interest in you. You need to capitalise on this interest by telling the reader something about you that makes you memorable and hopefully establishes a mutual interest.

This may include professional interests outside work, CSR and volunteering projects, industry renowned people with whom you have worked and anything of a celebratory nature that makes you stand out from the crowd.

EDUCATION AND QUALIFICATIONS

List of relevant professional training/qualifications with dates. For example if you have a degree, don't publish your GCSE results.

REFERENCES AND RECOMMENDATIONS

This is optional but wherever possible pick someone whom the reader knows or will be aware of.

[Reference and date of CV]

Appendix 2

Career development model - gap analysis

Fill in the form to identify the gaps to close to achieve your ideal role. Detailed instructions are below the model.

| Name | |
| Current Role | |

| Ideal role ? years out | |

Required Criteria

Click here to add a row to any part of this form.

Competency

	Ideal candidate	Ranking	Self Assessment	Gap analysis	
Qualifications					
				0	
				0	This colour denotes a score of between 2 and 4
				0	
				0	
Experience					This colour denotes a score of between 5 and 7
				0	
				0	
				0	
				0	This colour denotes a score of 8+
				0	
				0	
				0	
				0	
Skills					
				0	
				0	
				0	
				0	
				0	
				0	
				0	

Development Action Plan

To be completed following our next session

Type text here

Gap analysis instructions

Step One
Identify the job you would like to have in three to five years from today. Stipulate what your requirements are. For example: a twenty minute commute, I would like to work with an organisation that employs fewer than 100 people.

Ensure you consider the essential requirements and not just the role.

Step Two
Consider the best candidate for the role. Identify by qualification, experience and skills what "competencies" the very best candidate would need for that role. For example: a 1st class degree; ten years experience in the sector and marketing skills.

Step Three
Still using the ideal candidate; score the importance of each of those competencies using a scale of 1 to 10 in the Ideal Candidate column. For example: 1st class degree 9/10, ten years' experience 10/10.

Step Four
Take the score for each competency and rank it as follows:

Ranking
A   Absolutely essential
B   Highly desirable
C   Preferable

Review your scores and allocate to the three rankings on the basis of highest scores as A, mid-range scores B and lowest scores to C. If you have evenly scored the vast majority of items it may be necessary to score again on a plus and minus basis in order to get a distribution across the ranking.

So typically 10-8, score A; 7-5 score B; 4 or less C.

Step Five
Score your self against the ideal candidate by making an assessment of how closely you fulfil each competency requirement using the scale of 1 to 1. You can rank yourself more than, less than or the same as the ideal candidate, however there is normally a gap.

Step Six
Compare your rankings with that of the ideal candidate.

Step Seven
Interpret the results:
1. If you fail to match or better the ideal candidate on two or more of the A or B ranked requirements, you cannot get that job today.
2. Conversely, if you have no gaps or only one gap on the A or B competences you can get that job today.

Appendix 3
Proactive job search model

Just to remind you, here are the instructions from Chapter 7. This model is designed to help you effect introductions via your network to the points of purchase within target organisations.

You may find an excel spread-sheet works well for you to do the following:

- Identify the organisations likely to hire people with your skill set. If you group these organisations in threes you will have enough competitor information to have a meaningful discussion with any of them.
- Consider the characteristics of the sort of company you would like to work for and where you would do well.
- Identify the point of purchase – the decision-maker – not the HR department, they are the gatekeepers.
- Find out what can you about them – network, use your sources, LinkedIn, reference materials.
- Make notes of how and when you contact them.
- List and date all follow up actions.

On the second half of the spread-sheet, list your network and do the following:

- List your friends and contacts, their organisations and contact details.
- Segment your network on the basis of the strength of your relationship and the power of influence of your contact.
- Consider what you want to ask them and how to phrase the question.

Build your network with as many people as possible looking for you and let contacts know you're around and available.

Proactive job search model:

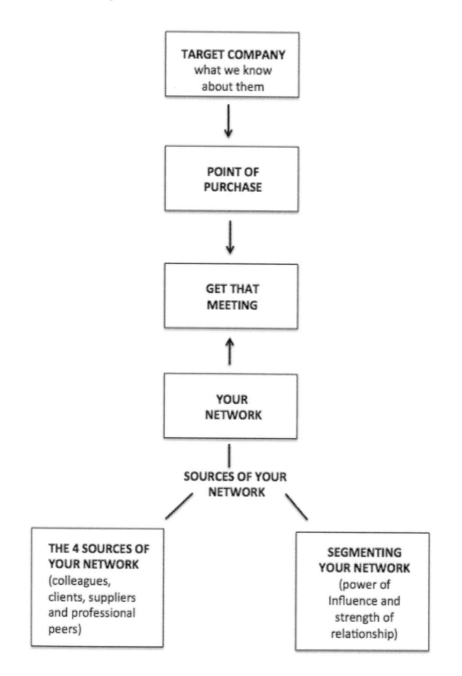

TARGET COMPANY
what we know
about them

↓

POINT OF
PURCHASE

↓

GET THAT
MEETING

↑

YOUR
NETWORK

SOURCES OF YOUR
NETWORK

THE 4 SOURCES OF
YOUR NETWORK
(colleagues,
clients, suppliers
and professional
peers)

SEGMENTING
YOUR NETWORK
(power of
Influence and
strength of
relationship)

References

Buckingham, Marcus and Clifton, Donald: *Now, Discover Your Strengths*

Buckingham, Marcus and Coffman, Curt: *First Break All the Rules*

Carnegie, Dale: *How to Win Friends and Influence People*

Covey, Stephen: *The Seven Habits of Highly Successful People*

Honey, Peter and Mumford, Alan: *Learning Style Preferences*

Hughes, Damian: *Liquid Thinking*

Isaacson, Walter: *Steve Job, Exclusive Biography*

Jeffers, Susan: *Feel the Fear and Do it Anyway*

Kolb, David: *Experiential Learning: Experience as the source of learning and development*

Lombardo, Michael M. and Eichinger, Robert W.: *The Leadership Machine*

Maxwell Maltz: *Creative Living for Today: The magical power of self-image psychology and psycho-cybernetics*

Orwell, George: *Animal Farm*

Schein, Edgar: *Career Anchors*

Schelling, Thomas C.: *Enforcing Rules on Oneself*, Journal of Law, Economics & Organization, Vol.1, No.2 (Autumn 1985)

Seligman, Martin: *Positive Psychology*

Smart, Brad: *Topgrading*

University of Michigan Business School: *Reflected Best Self*